If God is everywhere

why can't I find Him?

If God is
everywhere

why can't
I find Him?

Kimberly Sadler

LIVING INK BOOKS

First printing—March 2005

Cover designed by ImageWright, Inc., Chattanooga, Tennessee
Interior design and typesetting by Reider Publishing Services,
    West Hollywood, California
Edited and Proofread by Agnes Lawless, Dan Penwell, Sharon Neal,
    and Warren Baker

Printed in Canada
11 10 09 08 07 06 05 –T– 8 7 6 5 4 3 2 1

To my husband, Jim,
in whose faith, forgiveness, and love I find God.

CONTENTS

Acknowledgments   ix

Preface   xi

Introduction   xv

1   GOD AS CREATOR   1
Finding God in Our Chaos

2   GOD AS REDEEMER   19
Finding God in Our Mistakes

3   GOD AS PRESERVER   37
Finding God in Our Weariness

4   GOD AS PROVIDER   51
Finding God in Our Needs

5   GOD AS DEFENDER   65
Finding God in Our Battles

6   GOD AS TEACHER   79
Finding God in Our Confusion

7   GOD AS KING   95
Finding God in Our Hearts

ACKNOWLEDGMENTS

With *deepest gratitude to:*

My family for their endless encouragement, patience, and understanding during this book's creation,

Suzanne Fox, my consultant and fellow journeyman without whom this book simply would not be,

Pastor Bob Burridge for laying the theological groundwork for this project,

Pastor Jeff Birch for overseeing its construction,

Cheri Cowell, Evie Birch, Linda Toft, Betty Selig, Pastor Howard Alperin, Patti Sapp, and Nancy Cox, whose stories are included in this book, making it a far richer display of God's glory than I ever could have made it alone,

My dear and faithful friends at Spruce Creek Presbyterian Church and throughout the kingdom for their tireless and prayerful support in the life of this project and its author,

Peter Sprague of Corporate Training Partners for keeping me focused and accountable,

Agnes Lawless, a superb copyeditor, who helped make my words flow even better than I imagined they could,

Dan Penwell, my editor and my friend. God gave you ears to hear my heart. My thanks now and always to you and AMG Publishers for listening, and

My God who continues to teach me who he is and where he can be found.

PREFACE

LESS THAN A MINUTE after I electronically submitted this manuscript to my publisher on deadline, our doorbell rang. It was Katy. She and her mother Allison were early for her bridal shower in our home that evening, but they needed to discuss something important with me before the other guests arrived.

Standing on the beachside in a stiff southeastern breeze, my future daughter-in-law turned to her mother and me. "I know it's a lot to ask, but unless we move our wedding up by four days and get married tomorrow instead of Saturday, I'm afraid we won't be able to have the ceremony on the beach. They're saying that Hurricane Frances is going to hit the coast sometime between Friday and Sunday." Katy shook her head. "I haven't told James about my idea yet. He'll be shocked, but I'm sure he'll understand and agree. Do you think we can pull everything together in the next twelve hours?"

Six months earlier while home for the holidays, our oldest son, James, had proposed to Katy on the beach by moonlight. Since then, both had set their hearts on a barefoot wedding by the water's edge. I'd grown to love Katy and wanted nothing more than to help make her dream come true. "Of course we can pull it together in time! Your mom and I will do whatever needs to be done. And James will be thrilled to become your husband a few days ahead of schedule," I assured her. "After all, what's a little more chaos, right?" The three of us laughed. But we had no idea just how much chaos was headed our way.

On Wednesday, September 1, 2004, God gave James and Katy the perfect beach wedding. On Saturday, God gave Hurricane Frances permission to make landfall along the east coast of Florida. Her assault lasted thirty-six hours in Daytona Beach where we live. Along with countless others, we lost our roof and suffered major flooding and subsequent damage. My husband Jim, James, Katy, our younger son John, our two dogs, and I lived in and out of our garage and slept on concrete floors for several days. Some areas were without power for more than two weeks. Ice became more precious than gold, and the terms "hunker down" and "feeder bands" are now considered normal conversational phrases. Along its path, damage estimates from Frances reached into the billions, and those who lost loved ones in the storm are still reeling. Yet at this writing in September, 2004, another major hurricane is bearing down on Florida's east coast and is expected to strike a powerful blow in less than seventy-two hours. I confess I'm trying hard to remember who God really is so I can find him in the midst of the chaos right now.

Before I wrote this book, I was not fully aware of how easy it is to lose sight of God. As most of us do, I have a tendency to forget what he looks like and who he really is. So when the inevitable challenges of chaos, mistakes, weariness, fear, and discontent come along, we trust in far lesser things to see us through—like self-reliance, self-redemption, relationships, and personal agendas. All fall short. To make matters worse, most of us have neither the time nor the opportunity to sharpen our view of God through prolonged theological studies.

For these reasons, *If God Is Everywhere, Why Can't I Find Him?* is nervously and prayerfully offered—nervously because of God's vastness and sheer majesty. That I would know anything about him is absurd apart from his forgiveness, mercy and grace toward me through his Son, my Savior Jesus Christ. And prayerfully because I've tried to present Scripture's teaching, along with relevant life stories as a means by which God will reveal himself and cause us to remember who he is so we can find him in the thick of life. Even in a hurricane.

INTRODUCTION

"If you look for me in earnest,
you will find me when you seek me."

JEREMIAH 29:13

SOONER OR LATER, it happens to all of us. We walk out of stores and into parking lots and can't remember where we left our cars. Trying not to look obvious, we nonchalantly meander between aisles searching for familiar front bumpers or rear license plates. But by the end of our second lap around the lots behind our shopping carts full of groceries, even casual observers catch on.

When the stuff of life crowds our ability to remember, we laugh about losing our keys, our glasses, or our cars. But the all too real impact of life's hectic schedules, commitments, and unexpected crises poses a serious threat to our well-being: It jeopardizes our ability to keep an eye on what's really important.

We can even lose God in the turmoil, anxiety, fatigue, and confusion of our overloaded lives. We may try to change that by reading books on how to be better Christians. We go to retreats to recharge our spiritual batteries or do Bible studies on what makes us more godly.

I've done these things, too—and more—in hopes of getting back to God when I've lost sight of him in the thick of everyday life. While such things are not without merit, I've discovered that finding him again isn't as much about doing as it is about being aware of who he is and how he fulfills his unique roles in our lives.

Being aware of God is not difficult when we know what he looks like. Just like anyone else, he has distinct attributes and characteristics that make him identifiable. When we know what those are, it is easier to recognize him and find him again when he has temporarily faded from view.

God's roles and the ways in which he fulfills them are unique as well. As Creator, he manages the chaos in our lives. As Preserver, he sustains us and gives us true rest in life's craziness.

Knowing who God is, what his roles are, and how he fulfills them helps us to know what he looks like and where he can be found in the first place. But what if we're not sure about these things or need to be reminded of them? Where do we find the time and energy to clarify our understanding of who God really is?

There are seasons for everything, a time for every event under heaven (Eccles. 3:1). We go through seasons of having the time, energy, and opportunity for in-depth Bible study and rich moments of prayer and reflection. For the most part, these times are marked by abundant spiritual growth and forward motion. But we also have seasons filled with challenges and distractions. Day-to-day chaos, sudden crises, and unexpected responsibilities are potential traps that keep us from moving ahead spiritually. Even then, we need to keep our sights set on God. But how?

When my grandfather's old Jeep used to get stuck in soft sand on the way to his favorite fishing spot, he didn't panic. He simply put one foot on the gas pedal and the other on the clutch and rocked his Jeep back and forth in the sandy ruts until it climbed out of the trap. "Sometimes you've got to back up to go forward," he'd say.

It's that way in my spiritual life, also. When the time, energy, and opportunity to do even the routine things seem to elude me, I need to reconsider the way I think about growing. When life's demands, like sandy ruts, bog me down from finding God, one way to get moving again is to go back to the basics of who he really is.

If God has slipped from your view again (or you need to find him for the first time), listen to his encouraging instructions shared through the Old Testament prophet: "If you look for me in earnest, you will find me when you seek me" (Jer. 29:13).

As this passage reminds us, God is findable. He's not hiding from us. We can have a sense of expectancy when we look for him, a quiet confidence that we won't come back alone. When we're serious about finding God in our lives, his distinctive nature is distinguishable from the crowd. In a world of false gods competing for our time and attention, it's reassuring to know that we won't confuse God with a stranger as long as we know and remember what he looks like.

Going back to the basics of who God is and how he fulfills his unique roles in our lives equips us to better recognize him every day. As you read through the section below, prayerfully imagine how your life might be different if you were more aware of God's presence as your.

- **Creator.** His power and authority steers us through life's fiercest storms and around situations not designed for our good and his glory. Even in the midst of our chaos, God's love and sovereign rule whispers peace.

- **Redeemer.** His death on the cross for our sakes was rooted in love, not obligation. As human beings, we make mistakes, but God extends his gracious gift of forgiveness and loves us just as we are.

- **Preserver.** He gives us strength for our journeys and rest for our souls. In our weariness, God calls us to himself by his Spirit and through his Word where we find restoration and refreshment.

- **Provider.** He not only meets our needs but also satisfies our hearts' longings for wholeness and contentment.

- **Defender.** Whether we're in conflict with others or with our own selves, we can take hold of his promises and gain courage because God fights for us in our harshest battles.

- **Teacher.** He possesses all knowledge and wisdom and leads us into his truth that cuts through the darkest confusion. He makes things clear for us so we can see where we need to go in life and how to get there.

- **King.** He expresses his will on earth and in our lives through justice, mercy, forgiveness, and love. As his sovereign rule brings blessing to our lives, our hearts worship before him.

Setting aside impossible schedules, tough responsibilities, and inevitable trials isn't an option for most of us . . . but finding God in the thick of them is. I wrote this book out of my own personal struggles to regain and retain my awareness of him. Even though I still don't do it perfectly, I find it helpful to focus on the basics of who God really is in order to see him more clearly in everyday life. I pray that God uses this book to help you do just that.

1

GOD AS CREATOR
Finding God in Our Chaos

*"I am leaving you with a gift—peace of mind and heart.
And the peace I give isn't like the peace the world gives.
So don't be troubled or afraid."*

JOHN 14:27

 WHEN I WAS SEVENTEEN, I drove from Washington, D.C., to Daytona Beach, Florida, in search of my future. I'd graduated from high school a year early and was eager to find out how I was going to become the person I wanted to be.

The events of the 1960s and 1970s influenced my view of the future. The war in Vietnam and the Watergate scandal dominated the media and America's dialog with itself. But the women's liberation movement spoke loudest to me, not because it echoed my thoughts on womanhood, but because it didn't.

I admired my girlfriends who were anxious to shatter glass ceilings in the corporate world, and I sympathized with every woman who needed or wanted to work outside the home. But I wanted nothing more than to be a wife and a stay-at-home mom. I knew my aspiration was politically incorrect, but it was the only one I'd ever had. So when Jim, my childhood sweetheart, asked me to marry him in the winter of 1979, I was overjoyed.

Marriage felt right to me. It was easy to fall under my husband's love and care. By my midthirties, I was the mother of two sons and the wife of a fast-track, U.S. Air Force officer. Life was in full gear.

Jim traveled a lot in his job. Some trips kept him away for weeks at a time, forcing me to run things at home. In his absence, I was mother and father to our boys, ace auto mechanic, appliance repairman, spiritual leader, pediatrician, chauffeur, cook, and T-ball advisor. Whenever things got too much for me, I took comfort in knowing that Jim would eventually come home and calm the craziness.

I depended on Jim's quiet yet powerful strength. Whenever storms blew through our lives, I ran for cover under his counsel, his perspective, his embrace. He held me steady and steered me straight no matter how high the seas or how low my outlook. I looked to him to keep our world in order, to bring peace to its chaos.

The house was peaceful on an April morning when Jim came into the kitchen and asked, "Hey, Hon, what's this?" pointing to a small lump under his left jawbone.

At first I couldn't see anything. "Come over here to the light," I said, using my motherly voice.

Jim placed my finger on the lump. "It wasn't there yesterday," he said.

"I'm sure it's nothing, but I'll call the doctor to see if he wants you to take something for it."

Five weeks and three rounds of antibiotics later, the lump in Jim's neck had tripled in size, and the swelling was obvious. We tried to make light of it, but we both knew what the other one was thinking.

Our doctor referred us to a specialist who ordered several scans of Jim's head and neck. At our first appointment, we sat like scared children, listening numbly to the test results.

"It doesn't make sense, Jim," the surgeon said. "You just don't fit the profile. You're young, strong, and healthy in every other way. Typically, someone with throat cancer is a smoker or heavy drinker. But you're neither, yet something is there. And whatever it is, it has to come out. I'll do a biopsy during the surgery, and then we'll know exactly what we're dealing with."

Five days later, Jim was admitted to the hospital for a one-hour procedure that took nearly four. When his surgeon finally emerged from the operating room to tell me what the biopsy revealed, no words were necessary. Even from a distance, his eyes told me everything I needed to know.

"It's not good, Kim," he confirmed with a soft, low voice. "It's not what I expected to find. The mass in Jim's neck was large and malignant. It's an aggressive cancer. I had to do a radical neck dissection. We removed the tumor, lymph nodes, jugular vein, and most of the large muscle on the left side of his neck. I did a lot of biopsies. I have to get back to the operating room. We must identify the primary site. It doesn't make sense . . ."

In that moment, nothing felt familiar. It was as though I wasn't me anymore. All reference points disappeared. My heart flailed wildly, desperately searching for something to hold on to. "Oh God, tell me this isn't happening," I pleaded. I felt like a stone dropping through space. Faster and faster . . . everything swirling out of control. No peace. No order; only chaos.

Stunned by the news, family members staggered to their feet from their waiting-room chairs. One by one, they held me and cried. In many ways, Jim had been like a son and a brother to them for more years than he and I had been married. I was only fourteen when they met him for the first time, and he was a freshman in college. My family fell in love with him immediately, just like I did.

In spite of their attempts to comfort me, my heart instinctively reached out for Jim the way it always did when I was confused, afraid, or in pain. But for the first time in twenty-two years, he was nowhere to be found. The one who'd always been there to reassure me was far beyond my reach, leaving me disoriented and alone. From the chaos in my soul, I cried out, "God, are you there?"

After two days of reviewing their findings, Jim's doctors rendered a stage-four diagnosis of squamous cell carcinoma, one of cancer's most aggressive forms. I listened in disbelief as they explained details of the grueling chemotherapy and radiation treatments facing Jim. *How would he survive this horrific ordeal?* I wondered. *How would I?*

Jim's hospital room was ordinary, but the hours I spent there at his bedside were not. He was still my husband, but I hardly recognized him. He looked smaller and fragile. His hair was mussed and dull, and I wondered if he would lose it during chemo. His youthful face now looked old, drawn, and ashen.

Amputation patients experience "phantom limb syndrome," an eerie sense that their missing limbs are still there. If I closed my eyes and thought of Jim the way he used to be, I could almost feel his powerful embrace, even though circumstances cut him off from me.

Away from the hospital, life also ran amuck. Many things needed to be done right away. Phone calls to family and friends to let them know the latest on Jim. Hours on the computer to research alternative cancer treatments. Insurance matters to resolve. Time with our boys, who struggled to accept their dad's situation. And all the million-and-one other details that made up our lives throughout our twenty-two years of marriage.

Just as when Jim's job called him away, I was suddenly responsible for the oversight of our lives. Only this time when he came home, I would have no refuge from the storm.

The schedule for Jim's cancer called for two and a half months of chemotherapy once a week and heavy radiation to his torso every day. After that, doctors predicted a lengthy recovery period. Some patients in the same program took as many as six months to get back to normal.

Because of the challenges we faced, I surrounded myself with comforting people and things. I asked one friend to call every morning to see how the night went and another to call in the evening to make sure we got through the day. My pile of books and magazines stretched up to the ceiling. Some days I lingered while caring for Jim because it offered the safety of routine.

All these things could be innocent coping mechanisms. But I knew they would only tide me over until Jim had a lull in his misery. Then I would once again search for my equilibrium in his touch, his words.

In the beginning, Jim could speak. He eventually lost his voice for three months due to radiation burns on his vocal chords and throat. While he could still talk, I asked him to tell me things like, "It's all going to be okay," and "Don't worry; I'm here." It worked, but only for a while.

Outwardly, I kept my chin up, but inwardly I unraveled. I couldn't eat or sleep. My temper was set with a hair trigger, and my patience level hovered near empty. One minute I hated Jim for being sick, and a moment later I wept with longing to love him as before. My strength was sucked out of me. Within a month, I was living on coffee and sleeping pills.

Late one night after getting Jim settled, I wandered onto our back patio to get away from the suffering. The air was mild, and a cricket serenade played in the distance. I looked up at the night sky where a million stars hung, shining to their hearts' content.

Even though they were busy, each star seemed to be resting. They weren't darting back and forth across the heavens, clinging to one another, or shaking from shine stress. They just hung there being peaceful. "I wish I could do that," I whispered.

Since it was still pleasant outside, I lay down on the patio and thought more about the stars. They reminded me of Job, the Old Testament saint caught in difficult circumstances and the sovereignty of God.

To make sense out of chaos and restore order in his life, Job wrestled with his painful situation. He even questioned God's authority and integrity in his conversations he had with friends.

God overheard them and asked Job a few choice questions of his own: "Who is this that questions my wisdom with such ignorant words? Brace yourself, because I have some questions for you" (Job 38:2, 3).

Lying on my patio, I remembered the first few inquiries God directed Job's way. "Where were you when I laid the foundations of the earth? Tell me, if you know so much. Do you know how its dimensions were determined and who did the surveying? What supports its foundations, and who laid its cornerstone as the morning stars sang together and the angels shouted for joy?" (Job 38:4–7).

Thinking of these verses, I felt crushed. In my frenzy to find peace in life's chaos, I'd done exactly what Job did. I'd lost sight of God as Creator, and in so doing, I'd also over-looked some fundamental truths.

- God called everything into being out of chaotic nothingness by the sheer power of his word. "The LORD merely spoke, and the heavens were created. He breathed the word, and all the stars were born. . . . For when he spoke, the world began! It appeared at his command" (Ps. 33:6, 9).

  God has so much power and authority that when he spoke, things that didn't even exist listened and obeyed. Theologian R. C. Sproul said that there are no maverick molecules—everything, seen and unseen, answers to God. That means he controls whatever is in the universe or in our lives. At times the world might look like it's in chaos, but from God's perspective there's no such thing.

- God knows all things about all things, but he doesn't know them the way you and I do. We're limited in what we know and how we know it, whereas God's knowledge is perfect and complete. His thoughts are completely different from ours, and his ways are far beyond anything we can imagine. In the same way that the heavens are higher than the earth, his ways are higher than ours (see Isa. 55:8, 9).

  Not only does God know all about everything that is, has been, or will be, but he also knows about everything in every possible way. He's never surprised, never in the dark, and never needs do-overs because he messed up the first time.

- God is present in all places at all times all at once. There isn't anyplace we can go that he isn't already there. If we went up into the heavens, we'd find him. If we went down to the depths of the earth, he'd be there. On the wings of the sunrise or across the farthest sea, he's there waiting to guide us and hold us (see Ps. 139:7–10).

  Not bound by space or time, God is eternal. There is no time when he has not been. He is everywhere at every moment. So when we think we're alone in the thick of crises—we're not. God is there.

That night on the patio, God reminded me of what I'd forgotten about him. For the first time in my life, I understood what the stars have known all along: When we view anything or anyone other than God as Creator, we cannot find true peace. When I put Jim in the place of the Creator, I learned how fragile even the strongest earthly support can be. Many people place money in the Creator's role, relying on it as though it were the source of all pleasure and safety. For some of us, our children seem to *create* our lives. It doesn't matter which false Creator we rely on—it just doesn't work.

Many of us instinctively look earthward for stability when things get off balance. What props will hold us up? Who has what we need? How can we overpower the chaos? Yet even the most powerful ship can't subdue an angry ocean. In heavy seas it gets tossed around as if it's made out of matchsticks.

From training and experience, the ship's captain knows to rely on one thing to take his ship through a storm. Only the rudder can hold his ship steady and steer her straight in the roughest water.

Like the sea captain, we know we're going to encounter storms; they're facts of life. We're foolish if we don't rely on a rudder to hold us steady and steer us in the right direction when a gale hits. We need to remember that God is the Creator—he's the rudder that steers us into his peace.

God's peace isn't a feeling we get because external chaos disappears. It's what happens when we say, "In this situation, I'm agreeing that God is Creator. He's in control. He knows how to care for me, and he will not leave me alone."

The peace God gives is different from what the world offers. The world's peace is temporary and based on circumstances. God's peace is based on the truth that he is omnipotent (all-powerful), omniscient (all-knowing), and omnipresent (present everywhere). And that never changes. When our hearts grasp this, something transpires in our souls. The *something* is what the Bible calls God's peace—an outcome that stands guard over our hearts and minds to protect them from the effects of being thrown about by heavy circumstances (see Phil. 4:7).

Years ago, I accompanied our son's Cub Scout pack to a large water park for their annual summer outing. Kids being kids, they made a beeline to the most impressive ride first. I'm not big on rides since motion is a problem for me. But this ride was an enclosed, twisted, tangled tube that started nearly one hundred and fifty feet up in the air and ended in the middle of a lake. *Well, I do love to swim,* I thought.

Silly as it may sound to those with more daring personalities, no words describe the horror I experienced inside the Blue Twirly slide. Because the initial drop was so steep, my speed hit somewhere near fifty miles per hour in the first three seconds of descent. Panic set in, and I tried to stop myself by pressing my hands and feet against the walls. How did I know flesh peels off at that speed?

With every neck-breaking twist and turn, I shot into the next loop even faster than I'd entered the one before. I had no idea which way was up nor how much further I had to go. I thought I might have a heart attack if the ride didn't end soon. The sound of rushing water, coupled with my blood-curdling screams, produced a deafening echo that I can still hear in my head.

But would you believe, in the midst of that self-induced panic, I remembered that God was with me and was in control? I did! And when that thought flashed into my mind, I relaxed. Sure, I still hated being in the moment, but at least I knew I'd survive it.

Agreeing with truth doesn't mean we deny chaos. It means we acquiesce to God's ability to sustain us in it. The captain doesn't pretend that the waves aren't huge when he sees them crashing over the deck of his ship. He rests in knowing he has a rudder that will steer him to port. Likewise, I couldn't ignore the fact that I was ripping though the Blue

Twirly slide. But when God reminded me who he is, my fear subsided. In both instances, the effect of truth is peace.

Like a rudder, remembering God as Creator brings serenity. It steadies us in chaos and keeps us on course emotionally. When Jim was diagnosed with cancer, every part of me flew out of control. Our doctor offered me anti-anxiety medication. He assumed I couldn't make it through the cancer experience without something to buffer the stress, fear, and confusion that were sure to come.

The doctor was right. I couldn't. I took the medicine for a while, and it was helpful. But learning to recognize God's presence in my circumstances as Creator eventually brought peace to my soul and freedom from fear.

Learning to recognize God as Creator works itself out over the course of a lifetime. It's part of our sanctification. Ultimately, it's God's responsibility, but we should avail ourselves of his means of grace to strengthen us for the journey.

The Bible, one of God's provisions, is filled with examples of his people learning about who he is. His role as Creator is no exception. Take the disciples' infamous boat ride with Jesus, for example:

One day Jesus said to his disciples, "Let's cross over to the other side of the lake." So they got into a boat and started out. On the way across, Jesus lay down for a nap, and while he was sleeping the wind began to rise. A fierce storm developed that threatened to swamp them, and they were in real danger.

The disciples woke him up, shouting, "Master, Master, we're going to drown!"

So Jesus rebuked the wind and the raging waves. The storm stopped and all was calm! Then he asked them, "Where is your faith?"

And they were filled with awe and amazement. They said to one another, "Who is this man, that even the winds and waves obey him?" (Luke 8:22–25)

So often, God uses chaos to teach us who he is. In the disciples' case, the storm's turmoil on the lake and in their hearts served as a perfect backdrop to demonstrate the Lord's power. If there had been no storm, the disciples might not have realized that as Creator, God the Son had dominion over creation. In the same way, we don't look for unruly circumstances in life, but they show up—rebellious children, unfaithful spouses, lost jobs, health problems, aging parents.

We can be certain that as God used chaos to teach the disciples . . .

He uses chaos to teach us that he is in control. We're not.

He sees the future. We can't.

He knows what's best for us. We don't.

In just a few words, the apostle Paul assured fellow believers in Rome that no matter how rambunctious life may become at times, God causes everything to work together for the good of those who are called according to his purpose (see Rom. 8:28). Storms will come at us, but when we remember that God can orchestrate them for our benefit, we have peace.

For me, it's still difficult to look at Jim and not want to feel peace the easy way, even if it's counterfeit. Jim's voice has come back, though it's not the same. Neither is his touch or perspective; cancer changes everything. But he's alive for now and doing well. Naturally, it's tempting to cling to him the way I used to. But I don't. I know that no matter how important he is in my life, it's not his job to conquer chaos for me or to give me peace.

My thinking has shifted in other areas as well. Now I look at a tree and think, *God made this tree and the leaves, adding color and texture to them. He causes rain to fall that nourishes the tree, causing it to grow so birds can find shelter in its branches. Then he made shade to cover the ground. How amazing.* Before Jim's cancer, I don't think I would have noticed.

As you continually learn what God looks like, you'll find him more easily when you look in the right places, like chaos. You can find his peace in knowing that he is the Creator and therefore in control. This becomes your rudder; you rely on it to steer you straight.

No situation is too difficult that God cannot sustain you in it. No circumstance is so complex that God cannot see you through it. No trial, no problem, no event is greater than our God—our Creator—who loves you and works all things to his glory and your good.

AND THERE HE WAS . . .

by Christine Casselberry

My early childhood was nearly idyllic, but that didn't last. By the time I was thirteen, I walked on eggshells, afraid that a single word spoken the wrong way might lead to an emotional eruption. Many of my parents' conversations dissolved in angry outbursts and tears. I watched as the chasm between them deepened and as unmet expectations grew an emptiness within them that the other could not fill.

My father dealt with what was happening by staying late at work each day. When he came home at night, my mother was often sleeping. Her sleep was a good thing because then my father and I had a little peace.

Mother grew more emotionally unstable and withdrawn as the months passed. My father, unable to handle the situation, became childlike, told off-color jokes, and drew attention to himself. My mother, too, became more childlike. She hung out with my friends and dressed more like a teenager than a parent. Out of necessity, I assumed the role of an adult in our household as things worsened.

Like the child of an alcoholic, I never knew what I would encounter when I came home from school. I might find a fun-loving, childish mother, or perhaps she'd be in tears, claiming she couldn't go on with life. One time I found her slumped on the bed, having taken a half bottle of pain pills. When I called my dad at work, he told me to get Mom up, walk her around the house and make her drink a lot of water. I now know I should have called 911, but my family was living in the "no one should know our secrets" zone. Another time I found her in the neighborhood, wandering around in the rain, trying to gather her courage to jump in front of oncoming traffic.

Many nights I sat on the edge of my parents' bed, using the psychology I studied in women's magazines. I tried to help them see beyond their own views to the needs and feelings of the other. I sought guidance in books and TV talk shows, but above all, I sought God's guidance and comfort. He alone knew the things that happened behind closed doors in my home. He knew my parents and their individual longings and fears. He knew how to help my parents better than any magazine, book, or daytime talk show. He also knew me.

My girlfriends shared secrets and enjoyed sleepovers, but I never felt comfortable leaving my mother overnight or talking about the turmoil I lived in, except with one trusted friend. All the songs I grew up singing about Jesus being my friend and refuge in times of trouble now became my anthems. While my girlfriends argued with their friends, I grew to trust my best Friend as someone who was always there, always understanding, always trustworthy. I read in my Bible that he chose me, not as his servant, but as a friend, and that he loved me more than any girlfriend ever could (John 15:13–16).

Each day I showed a happy face at school and a confident and in-control face at home, but I was a frightened little girl underneath the facade. The more I tried to gain control over the chaos, the more unraveled my world became. My search for solutions to my parents' marital problems suffocated me.

In my nightly conversations with my best Friend, I shared about my day and how overwhelmed I felt. I told him about my fears of losing the safety net of my family, regardless of how torn that net appeared. Sometimes, I even yelled at God, knowing he was big enough to handle my anger and frustration.

In spite of my pain and confusion, I always ended my conversation by thanking God for faithfully being there and for hearing my prayers. I couldn't see the answers to my prayers, but I knew he was working on them. Maybe it was more of a desperate hope, but I didn't know what else to hope in. Although I longed to see my parents happy and at peace, they appeared headed for divorce, and I could do nothing to stop it.

Late one night as a thunderstorm brewed in the distance, I once again poured out my heart to my Friend. "God, I don't know how much more I can take! You know my heart and what I desire. Please take this pain from me." As I sobbed, I felt a peace wash over me, one that I'd never experienced before. God seemed to say, "I have heard you and will answer your prayers."

Things did not instantly improve, but I knew my best Friend had my parents, the situation, and me under his control. Hebrews 6:19 told me that Jesus was the anchor for my soul. Although the storm continued to rage, my soul was moored to a rock that never moved, and I found peace in my chaos.

God was the only refuge I could find in the storm that raged through my life. As he promised, Jesus was there through my parents' divorce, healing their hearts, minds, and emotions. By his grace he met their needs for companionship and love. Though they divorced one another, each later found someone to love and marry.

Peace finally came to our family, though not the way I expected. Sometimes Jesus calms the storms in our lives by providing miracles and answering prayers instantly. Other times he weathers the storms of chaos with us, helping us to trust him more deeply than before.

Now when storm clouds appear in my life, I know that Jesus is my refuge. He is my anchor to whom I can cling. Within his arms, I can rest as I hear him whisper, "Peace, be still."

2

GOD AS REDEEMER
Finding God in Our Mistakes

"I have swept away your sins like the morning mists.
I have scattered your offenses like the clouds.
Oh, return to me, for I have paid the price to set you free."

ISAIAH 44:22

 AS THE ECHO of harsh words and slamming doors subsided, I stood quietly and stared at the anonymous, hand-painted prayer scrawled on a small plaque that had hung on our bedroom wall for years. My tears kept me from seeing the words clearly, but it didn't matter. I knew them by heart—OH GOD OF SECOND CHANCES AND NEW BEGINNINGS, HERE I AM AGAIN.

Earlier in the evening, Jim and I were supposed to go out for dinner together. Because eating was still difficult for him, he preferred not to go to restaurants. But it was our twenty-third wedding anniversary, and he knew my heart was set on going to our favorite bistro for dinner and then to a bookstore around the corner for coffee. Just the two of us, doing what we used to do before cancer invaded our lives.

All afternoon, I felt like a schoolgirl getting ready for that one special date—excited and a little nervous. *I'll wear my red dress. No, I'll look thinner in the beige one. Wait . . . maybe I should wear something more casual,* I argued with myself in front of my opened closet door. I wanted Jim to like the way I looked, but seven months of wearing only caregiver blue jeans and T-shirts had obviously left me fashion-impaired. After nearly thirty minutes of indecision, I opted for black slacks and a jacket. Finally at ease with my choice of outfits, I headed for the shower armed with an array of shampoos and conditioners, lamenting my overgrown haircut.

Like most wives, I desire my husband's affection and approval. A well-placed compliment from Jim makes me feel like a million dollars and reassures me of his love. Likewise, to the degree I feel insecure about myself or the state of our marriage, I want to hear him say things like, "Wow, you look great!" "I admire the way you handled that situation," or "I'll love you no matter what."

Understandably, Jim's focus had not been on regular and romantic communication that reaffirmed his love for me. Surviving the emotional challenges that accompanied his cancer diagnosis took every ounce of energy and attention he could muster. Anxiety, depression, and fear were never far away from him. I fell heir to the same challenges. But for some reason, I also possessed a deep need for reassurance that I was still what he wanted after twenty-three years, two kids, and the twenty-five pounds that I couldn't seem to shake off.

For the most part, I suppressed my urge to engage Jim in deep, emotional discussions about loving reassurances while he was sick. I knew he had his own struggles to deal with. But his recent emotional return to our marriage, albeit partial, stirred my desire to feel loved and accepted. As I dressed and fussed feverishly with my hair for our special night out, I waited for Jim to say something like, "You look pretty," or "I'm glad you're my wife," but he didn't. Even when I fished for compliments, I came up empty.

I know I'm not perfect, but I've been a faithful wife and a good enough mommy. And I'm still here after all these years, I groaned under my breath. *What more do I have to do to get him to say he loves me?*

That night, my need for Jim's reassurance replaced the joy of celebrating our anniversary. Instead of sharing a quiet dinner, a cup of coffee, and memories with my husband, I accused him of not loving me enough when in fact he loves me better than any human ever has. Like most men, he simply forgot that a woman needs to be regularly told by her husband that she is loved, appreciated, and adored.

Having sufficiently damaged the evening, I stared at the wall plaque in our bedroom. With tears streaming down my cheeks, I confessed, "God, I did it again. I believed that outward things like my appearance, my behavior, and Jim's affirmation should shape my self-view. I know they're subjective and temporary, and I should never trust them to define me. Why can't I remember that my well-being as a wife rests in knowing that Jim loves me for who I am, not for what I do?"

Today I still struggle to believe that anyone can love me just as I am, even God. He is holy; his standards are high— I'm grossly unholy; my standards are only as high as I feel like reaching at any given moment. I shudder at the divine majesty and splendor of God when I read the psalmist's account,

> For who in all of heaven can compare with the LORD? What mightiest angel is anything like the LORD? The highest angelic powers stand in awe of God. He is far more awesome than those who surround his throne. O LORD God Almighty! Where is there anyone as mighty as you, LORD? Faithfulness is your very character. . . . Give honor to the LORD, you angels; give honor to the LORD for his glory and strength. Give honor to the LORD for the glory of his name. Worship the LORD in the splendor of his holiness. Psalms 89:6–8; 29:1, 2

Deep down, most of us know that we should try to please this holy and wonderful God by living according to his laws and his ways. In fact, we are created to do that very thing, but we don't. We rebel. Instead of living to please him, we live to please ourselves. We decide what's right and wrong. We decide what truth is. It's as though we become our own gods, each with our own way of doing things.

We might feel good about our efforts to live a good life. We might even gain the admiration of others. But the Bible says that if we fail to perfectly keep one of God's commandments—even if we only do it one time and ever so slightly—say with just a bad attitude toward someone or something, we fall short. And the penalty for that is death—spiritual separation from God in this life and the one to come (see Rom. 3:23; James 2:10).

We may not think too much about our rebellion against God, but he won't allow it to exist indefinitely. Ultimately, each person must pay the penalty for his or her rebellion. On the surface, this may seem unreasonable. How could a loving God judge people so harshly?

But the bigger question is this: How could a holy God love offensive people so much that he would personally pay the penalty for their rebellion, declare them nonoffensive and clean, wholeheartedly enter into relationships with them as their father, and bring them to life with hearts overflowing with gratitude for his mercy and forgiveness? Yet this is exactly what God did through his Son, Jesus Christ.

God moved us from where we were (offensive and separated from him) to where we are (forgiven and reconciled to him). This was the plan all along. God knew that while we still had the capacity to live his way, we no longer had the ability to do so. Since that day in Eden, our inclinations have not been to choose God. So Jesus did it for us. He lived the life we never could by keeping every one of God's commandments perfectly. He never had a wrong thought, an impure motive, a bad day. He never cheated, stole, lusted, or lied. He loved God and others perfectly, forgave everyone completely, and healed to the uttermost. He satisfied God's requirement to live his way all the time.

A person who lived so perfectly should receive accolades and honor from others. But that wasn't the case with Jesus. Instead of embracing him, the world rejected him. People preferred to keep living their own way rather than God's. So they killed Jesus in hopes of making the whole issue disappear.

Jesus' death was part of God's plan. Not only did he live the life we should have lived, but he died the death we should have died. In our place on the cross, he endured the full fury of God's judgment, vengeance, and wrath. It ripped through him on every level—body, mind, and spirit. Though he was innocent, Jesus became our substitute, paid the penalty we owed, and settled our account with God once for all. Jesus rendered our debt PAID IN FULL. We are forgiven.

But even that was not enough. God's plan also included our freedom from the forces that entice us to rebel in the first place, which ultimately lead to death. After Christ died on the cross, his resurrection three days later revealed his complete power over all opposing forces both seen and unseen. Not even death could hold him in the grave. God gives us this same power if we embrace what he has done through Christ on our behalf. And all of this because God loves us so much.

Why, then, do we often feel less like beloved children and more like orphans? We may say, "God, you feel so distant. When I manage to get close to you, I can't relax. I feel like I'm always coming up short. I try to do the right things, but just when I think I'm on track, something happens, and I'm back to square one again. I'm tired of wearing a mask to keep others from seeing my struggle. I feel like a hypocrite. Am I really your child? God, do you love me? God, are you there?"

Over coffee recently, I shared with a friend that I struggle to believe that I'm the girl Jim still wants. "When we were first married, it was easy to believe he loved me," I told her. "Everything was new. I was like a package he was opening for the first time, and he always seemed to like what he found inside. But as the years passed, his response toward me changed. To be fair, after two kids and all that goes along with motherhood, *intrigue* wasn't exactly my middle name."

I stirred cream into my coffee and gazed out the window. "So I started working hard to be what I thought made me attractive to him in the first place. Those extra pounds had to come off. Jim liked the outdoors, so I starting kayaking with him. I even considered rollerblading until a skating friend of mine fell and shattered her elbow. I read several books on love and marriage, and I re-enrolled in seminary to finish my degree."

My friend looked me in the eye. "And that wasn't enough?" she asked.

"I felt like my makeover was going pretty well," I said, "but Jim didn't do much to confirm my assessment. His references to my hard work were few, and he didn't say anything romantic very often. Then one day while I was cleaning up after breakfast, I found a note from him on the kitchen counter. It read,

MY DARLING WIFE, I LOVE YOU. ALWAYS HAVE. ALWAYS WILL. JIM.

I still have that note. When things aren't going right between us or I'm feeling vulnerable to self-criticism, I take it out of my drawer and read it again. Being reminded that I'm loved for who I am, not for what I do, sends my doubts and insecure thoughts right out the window."

You may have had a similar experience. In an attempt to win the love of people important to you—if not your mate, then perhaps your parents, children, or friends—you may have failed to recognize what was yours all along. They loved you no matter what. In your efforts to do what you thought made you appealing to them, you failed to experience their ability to love you in spite of your flaws, your mistakes, your human limitations. Like me, you may have worked so hard to be loved by them that you lost sight of who they really were—people who loved you just as you are.

Many of us make the same mistake in our relationships with God. We think we have to do things to make ourselves attractive to him—in order for him to accept us indefinitely, we have to keep him interested, engaged, and in love with us by living a list of do's and don'ts. The truth is, the harder we work at being attractive to God, the more we lose sight of him as our Redeemer—the One who loved us so much that even when we were still offensive to him, he died for us (see Rom. 5:8).

The reason we *perform* for God is that we forget why he loves us in the first place. We fail to look at both sides of Calvary. When we look at the cross, we see God's forgiveness. He put all our mistakes and sins on Christ, judged him guilty, and condemned him instead of us. Then Jesus died. In that way, God satisfied his own demand for justice: The penalty for sin was paid in full. But that's only half the story. God also put Christ's righteousness—every good and right thing he ever did or would do—on us, giving us his record instead of our own. Now when God looks at you and me, he sees Jesus instead. Theologians call this twist "double imputation" (see 2 Cor. 5:21).

If you've ever hiked long distances, you know how important it is to load your backpack evenly. Nothing makes walking more difficult than an off-balance pack. It throws your center of gravity from side to side, making your journey unpleasant and causing fatigue. Similarly, when we forget both sides of the cross—that we've been forgiven and declared righteous—we get thrown off balance spiritually. Instead of enjoying our journey with God, we grow weary and disheartened.

After a while, it's easy to tell when we've forgotten all aspects of our redemption. Instead of resting in our relationships with God, we're worried about making mistakes. And we're tired; trying to merit his love and approval is exhausting. Since it's impossible to satisfy his requirements for right living, our efforts to please him leave us feeling guilty instead of relieved.

We're right to cry out to God, "Lord, where are you?" The fatigue we feel from trying to please him in our own strength shuts our hearts down and cuts us off from enjoying him. Instead of confessing that God is good, we worry,

Am I okay? Then when we inevitably mess up, we feel condemned, not forgiven. *I'm a failure!* we tell ourselves. *God doesn't love me. He only loves people who get it right.* Before long, our fellowship with him is replaced by distance. Rather than running into his arms for reassurance, we avoid him. Our hearts grow cold and we wonder, *Am I even a Christian at all?*

If you're reading this book because you've lost sight of God in the chaos, confusion, and clutter of your life, there's a good chance you're already a Christian. If so, the thought of losing your salvation needn't taunt you. Consider what the Bible teaches about God's ability to preserve every person he saves.

In his address to Jewish leaders regarding his authority as Messiah, Jesus said, "My sheep recognize my voice; I know them, and they follow me. I give them eternal life, and they will never perish. No one will snatch them away from me, for my Father has given them to me, and he is more powerful that anyone else. So no one can take them from me. The Father and I are one" (John 10:27–30).

Later in the New Testament, the apostle Paul writes, "And I am sure that God, who began the good work within you, will continue his work until it is finally finished on that day when Christ Jesus comes back again" (Phil. 1:6). Our confidence in our eternal future must be rooted in God's power and promise to keep us in Christ.

The Bible also teaches that faith without works is dead. But the works it speaks of are those that are evident and flow naturally out of humble and grateful hearts already redeemed by God (see James 2:18, 22). Good works appear in our lives as proof of our salvation, never the cause of it (see 1 John 2:5).

We struggle with feelings of unworthiness and fear God's rejection because we forget how thorough his redemption is. We're not responsible for making and keeping ourselves clean. Rather, we need to take these comforting words to heart:

> Come now, let us argue this out, says the LORD. No matter how deep the stain of your sins, I can remove it. I can make you as clean as freshly fallen snow. Even if you are stained as red as crimson, I can make you as white as wool (Isa. 1:18).

On the cross, God through Christ made us right with himself. We are clean from the inside out, no longer offensive to him. Even the stains from the most horrible things we could ever do have already been washed away. Because of Jesus, we can go humbly into God's very throne room, knowing we're welcomed there as we confess our mistakes and find healing for our souls (see 1 John 1:9).

As wonderful as God's plan is, rejecting it is more common than we might think. At some time, haven't we all had thoughts like, "If I don't go to Sunday school, I'm not a good Christian." Or, "She's so involved in children's church. I ought to be more like her." Or how about, "I had my quiet time this morning, so I'm on track with God."

At the heart of this thinking is a prideful do-it-yourself approach to redemption. What we're saying is, "God, your plan was incomplete. I need to add my efforts, my works to what Jesus did on the cross so you'll love me enough to save me. I have a goodness of my own; part of me is above sin's reach." It's almost like saying, "God, I don't need you. I can redeem myself."

If you're old enough to remember grocery store trading-stamp programs, you've seen an excellent picture of true redemption. The can openers, blenders, and toasters at the redemption centers couldn't jump off the shelves and leave on their own. Someone had to redeem them and buy them back with the right number of filled trading-stamp books.

Defined as "to buy back, get back, recover as by paying a fee," the word *redeem* describes what Jesus did for us. He came to earth to buy us back from the penalty of sin. God gave Jesus and got us in return. Then he tucked us under his arm, so to speak, and walked out of the redemption center. We belong to him now.

We lose sight of God when we work hard to please him. Thankfully, he comes as Redeemer in the midst of our mistakes to remind us of all he's done through Christ on our behalf and to lift us out of our destructive self-righteous behaviors and attitudes. It might seem strange that we find God in our mistakes, but after all, it's because of our mistakes that he came to us in the first place. How wonderful that we can relax with God and be who we are—little children awkwardly learning to rest in his love.

Real redemption soothes and restores. The full truth of Calvary erases our guilt, melts our hearts, and reconciles us to God once for all. We no longer need to feel condemned, inadequate, or pressured to perform. Clothed in Christ's righteousness, our Redeemer loves and accepts us just the way we are.

Later that night, I skulked down the hallway and found Jim sitting in his recliner in our den. A small lamp on the end of the piano cast a soft glow.

"Please forgive me for ruining our evening," I said, still sniffling. "I know my insecurities steal so much from our marriage. I wonder if I'll ever get past them."

Jim just sat there, staring off into space. Had I gone too far this time? Had my words hurt him too deeply? *Say something!* I cried out in my heart.

Then a smile started at the corner of Jim's mouth and spread across his face. I wondered what he was thinking. He reached up from his chair, took my hand gently, and pulled me down on his lap. With eyes full of compassion and forgiveness, he looked at me and said softly, "I love you, Kim. Happy anniversary."

And There He Was . . .

by Evie Birch

Jesus once said I looked really good on the outside but was rotting away on the inside. Actually, he was talking about Pharisees, but what he said about them described me perfectly. On the outside, I had all the right appearances and religious activities going for me. As my age increased, so did the level of my Christian service. But on the inside, my rotting away was progressing, too. I not only was tired, frustrated, and unkind, but I was also worried, bitter, resentful, anxious, lonely, and self-occupied. A rising decline in my joy paralleled my increased Christian service, but by then I was addicted. Instead of using good works to serve God, I used them to serve myself.

At some point, my husband Jeff decided that we should go through a discipleship course for pastors and their wives. One of our first assignments was to submit our weekly schedules to our discipler. I got out the ruler and made a grid of my week that included time for God, my housework, husband, son, job, church, and people. It was, if I may say so, a piece of organizational genius. But our next phone appointment with our course discipler proved differently.

Jeff's schedule received glowing comments, but the discipler had only one thing to say about mine. "Evie, you hate God." What? Couldn't he read? Didn't he see all my "God time" neatly scheduled on my chart? I was indignant. I included all the priorities in my schedule that a good

Christian woman should have, and I had been to enough Bible studies to prove it. I began an elaborate defense of myself. But there it was again. "Evie, you hate God."

As the weeks progressed in our discipleship course, despite some intense hostility on my part, I began to see that yes, I did hate God. I truly was a Pharisee who did the right things for God to satisfy outward appearances but did not enjoy or want God on the inside in the deepest parts of my life.

The core of my rotting disease was that I thought I had done all the right actions to please God and that he owed me. As a result, deep ulcers of hurt ate away at me, and God wasn't healing them. Marriage wasn't the utopia my Bible study friends told me it was. In fact, it was hard work. Childbirth was a difficult experience for me, too. I was terribly sick for many months after our son was born. Because I was running a fever, I could not even hold him for several days or nurse him. My husband had to take over the major part of caring for our new infant. It was yet another major disappointment with God.

Then too, Jeff and I were living in an uncomfortable environment for me. I seldom felt safe when he was working at night. Life as a young pastor's wife in an older congregation was tough, and I was thin-skinned. Despite people, people, and more people in our lives and in our home, I was incredibly lonely. My list of misgivings toward God was long.

Thinking that the prescription for my malady was to convince God that he should like me and make life go my way, my to-do list of Christian works grew longer still. The verse, "Delight yourself in the Lord and he will give you the desires of your heart" (Ps. 37:4 NIV) meant to me that I do and God owes. I was like the older brother in the story of the prodigal son saying to his father, "Look at all the years I have slaved for you, and you never gave me a party!" In my life, I was doing the work, but I sure didn't see any balloons coming my way. I was undone and didn't know how to find God without the busyness. And furthermore, why should God want me anyway? I was a mess. My spiritual resume was getting me nowhere fast when God stepped in and showed me his plan.

If someone asked you, "What is the greatest need in your life?" how would you answer? It wasn't this way before, but I can now say that the greatest need in my life is not for temporal things to go the way I want. It is forgiveness—daily, ongoing forgiveness.

Instead of asking, *What would Jesus do?* Now I ask, *What has Jesus done?* Jesus lived and died to forgive me and to declare me righteous in God's sight. When God looks at me, he sees the beauty and righteousness of Jesus. It's not about me or my performance. It's all about Jesus and his performance on my behalf.

I used to shake an angry fist at God and tell him all I thought I deserved—when all I deserved was God's wrath. God answered my demands with his Son. Jesus' death and resurrection make it possible for me to live in God's presence no matter what I do or don't do.

Is it important to spend time with God, love my family, and serve my church? Absolutely! The problem is not such actions, but my motivation behind them. Good works become an idol when I use them to manipulate God into giving me what I want or to secure his love. The truth is, nothing can change my position with God. I am forgiven and loved because of Jesus.

Oh, about the party and the balloons. One of my favorite Bible verses is, "The Lord your God is with you, he is mighty to save. He will take great delight in you, he will quiet you with his love, he will rejoice over you with singing" (Zeph. 3:17 NIV).

I am completely redeemed already. Now there's the party!

3

GOD AS PRESERVER
Finding God in Our Weariness

"Come to me, all of you who are weary and
carry burdens, and I will give you rest."
MATTHEW 11:28

 IF YOU'RE A WOMAN, I don't need to tell you about feeling weary. You know it all too well. Many of us live near the verge of deep weariness much of the time, ready to topple over into the depths of exhaustion with only the slightest addition to our responsibilities. For me, the straw that broke the camel's back came when I decided to go to work part-time two years before Jim's cancer.

We weren't teetering on the edge of financial ruin, but Jim and I could feel our money getting tighter. With major house repairs, secondhand cars, and two teenage boys, our reserves were dangerously low, and we rarely had cash just for fun. We agreed that a little extra money each month would come in handy. So when a friend said she needed help at her store, my ears perked up.

Our oldest son, James, was almost in college, and our youngest, John, was about to start his freshman year in high school. Was it finally time to stretch my wings and leave the nest to help ease our growing financial burden? Besides, it was only a part-time position—twenty hours a week at the most, maybe thirty during the holidays.

I could juggle my family, my seminary studies, and a job, I told myself. It was simply a matter of managing my time. I wasn't a workforce veteran since I'd been a stay-at-home mom for most of our marriage, but I believed that running a household for twenty years had to be worth something. Overseeing a spouse, two kids, more cats and dogs than I cared to remember, pediatric appointments, carpool maneuvers, and countless basketball practices, band camps, and back-to-school nights must have taught me a few basic management skills. Besides, women everywhere go off to work every day.

At first, being out in the real world agreed with me. I learned the ropes at my friend's stationery shop without much trouble, and I enjoyed being with grown-ups. When I wasn't at the cash register or restocking shelves, I wrote and designed party invitations for clients. Scratching my creative itch felt good, and I often lingered after hours to put finishing touches on special orders. My boss was pleased with my performance, and so was I. If only things had been going as well at home.

Shortly after starting my job, I noticed a serious shortage in my time and energy after work. Even if I'd made it to the grocery store earlier in the day, cooking a decent dinner for my family challenged me. I grabbed my own meals on the run and skipped exercise. Keeping up with the laundry was out of the question. My crazy schedule, two boys, and a house full of pets made sure of that.

Time passed, but my struggle to find my groove as a working mom didn't. Fatigue and frustration spilled over into every area of my life. I couldn't get a handle on even the small things I used to do like get the kids to school and to ball practice on time.

For the most part, Jim and the boys adjusted to my new schedule. They were gracious about pitching in to help, but there were some things only I could do. Keeping up with my seminary studies was one of them. I did my best not to fall behind, but after only two months on the job, I had to withdraw from the program. I continued to lead a small women's Bible study, but in my heart I couldn't wait for the course to end so I'd be free from its extra responsibilities.

I felt sad and guilty. Shouldn't I of all people—a Bible study teacher and seminary student—find the time and energy to keep up with Christian disciplines? My quiet time with God had been reduced to whatever I could get in on my fifteen-minute drive to work in the mornings. Once in a while I skimmed the Scriptures, but my heart wasn't really in it. I went to church out of habit, thinking it was better than not going at all. But even there I was so tired that I struggled to keep my mind from wandering. I missed God.

It didn't take long to figure out that life was exhausting and distracting me. I was losing sight of everything important. My relationship with Jim suffered. Who feels like romance when you're dead on your feet? Except for watching my boys from the stands at their ball games, I rarely saw them until bedtime. They did their homework and played video games after dinner while I collapsed on the sofa.

I didn't want to admit it, but I was also losing sight of God. So I decided to do something to try to find him again. If I did that, maybe the rest of my life would fall in line, too, I hoped. At first, the solution seemed simple: Make a "get back to God" plan. To squeeze in more time for prayer and Bible reading each day, I set my clock for 5:00 a.m. instead of 6:00 a.m. What a painful mistake that was. I soon discovered the only thing I wanted to squeeze that early in the morning was my pillow.

Self-directed Bible study wasn't working too well, so I attended a church-sponsored theology class once a week. And if a women's conference or retreat came to town, I made sure I went. I talked a lot about God. I wrote a lot about God. I thought a lot about God. I worked hard to find him while I grew more exhausted each day. Eventually I couldn't sustain my pace any longer. With my energy and good intentions gone, I was right back where I started—weary and longing for God's presence but unable to find him.

Things finally changed shortly before Christmas, several months after I'd started my job. As usual more laundry needed washing than I cared to think about, but if anybody was going to have clean underwear the next day, I had to fire up the machines.

Max, our golden retriever, followed me through the rooms as I filled a basket of dirty clothes. Loaded down with jeans, T-shirts, towels, and socks, we headed to the laundry room where I sorted lights from darks and wondered why we could put a man on the moon but couldn't invent clothes that didn't get dirty.

Jim and the boys were out for a night of Christmas shopping, so the house was quiet except for the Boston Pops rendition of "Sleigh Ride" playing on the stereo. It was getting late, but the curtains on the laundry room's sliding glass door were still open. The night was clear and cold. Through the glass I watched smoke spiraling upward from the chimney on the house across the street.

Maybe it was the familiar Christmas music playing in the background or maybe it was my fatigue, but a sudden sadness came over me. The harder I tried to ignore it, the deeper it went until sometime between adding detergent to the washer for the second load of clothes and cramming the first load into the dryer, I started to cry. The strain of working part-time, caring for my family, and trying to keep God in sight was more than I could handle. I collapsed in a heap next to a mound of dirty clothes on the floor and sobbed. "God," I whispered. "I've lost you in the craziness of my life. I'm exhausted. Drained. Worn out. I can't keep going, but I have to. I'm stuck in a trap and don't have the strength to get out of it. Please, God, help me."

Regardless of who we are or where we live, duties in all shapes and sizes bombard us from the time we wake up in the morning until we fall asleep at night. In themselves, they're fairly benign. How else would anything ever get done? The problem is they don't attack alone.

What we need to protect our bodies from fatigue isn't hard to come by. A decent diet, quality sleep, and exercise go a long way toward replacing what the demands of life take from us. When we get those things, we feel better. A long, hot bath and a pint of ice cream work wonders, too.

But what about the tiredness that isn't erased by a long soak in the tub or a good meal? What about that "to the gut, at the core of your being" kind of tired that won't let up? What about weariness?

The word *weary* has an original meaning of "giddy" or "drunken." It's the idea of being upright but without the capacity to stand. Just a shell. Depleted. Exhausted. Ever feel that way?

Weariness isn't the kind of tired that comes from life's busyness. It's the result of bearing a heavy load of difficult circumstances that never seem to end. The source might be occupational demands, educational requirements, or the relentless challenge of balancing life's many commitments. It could be a marriage that lacks communication, passion, or respect; the behavior of a rebellious child; the ongoing grind of living from paycheck to paycheck; or memories of a painful past. Maybe disease, illness, or shame causes our weariness. Or maybe something as simple as a part-time job upsets the balance of everything else.

Whatever the load is that causes our weariness, we can't carry it by ourselves forever. Oh, we might manage to keep going for a while, hanging on by a thread. But God wants us to experience the wonder of his preserving power, refreshment, and restoration. He wants us to do more than just get by.

When we're already weary, the last thing we need is to add something else to our load. Thankfully, finding true rest has nothing to do with that. Rather, it has to do with being . . . being aware that God is our Preserver. In the midst of our weariness, God calls to us with the promise of rest for our souls in Jesus Christ.

Jesus knows about weariness. In his humanity, he met with folks, traveled incessantly, went without sleep, went without food, performed miracles, taught, prayed, preached, debated, dodged dissidents, and dashed demons. Finally, he carried the burden of sin to the cross where his Father unloaded the full weight of his holy wrath on him.

Jesus also knows about rest. He was there in the beginning when it was commanded at creation (see Gen. 2:1–3). God was not tired from all his work, but he established rest to illustrate what belongs to us now and in eternity: relief from our burdens and the suffering they bring to our lives.

But relief comes in different ways. The Bible does not promise that God will subdue every difficult situation we go through or flatten every mountain we climb in order to keep us from weariness. Therefore, it must mean that he sustains us during the challenging times in such a way that they don't break us down for good. But how?

Then Jesus said, "Come to me, all of you who are weary and carry heavy burdens, and I will give you rest. Take my yoke upon you. Let me teach you, because I am humble and gentle, and you will find rest for your souls. For my yoke fits perfectly, and the burden I give you is light" (Matt. 11:28–30).

In ancient times, yokes joined beasts closely together to ease their burden and keep their path straight. When we're yoked with Jesus, he shares the weight we pull, and we walk closely beside the One who is always *on track*.

When we stay close to Jesus, we learn to walk as he walked—relying completely on God to sustain us. We need not fear ridicule when we ask him to teach us to depend on God. On the contrary, he promises to teach us when we say, "Jesus, I don't know how to live your way, depending only on our Father. Please show me."

When we look carefully at how Jesus lived in the thick of life, we see his total dependence on God. He never relied on anything or anyone else to sustain or renew him. Accomplishing God's will nourished him (see John 4:34). Listening to and watching what the Father did gave him direction (see John 5:19, 20). God's sovereignty was the lens through which he viewed all matters of life, even those difficult to understand (see John 9:3). He trusted the Father to care for people most precious to him (see John 17). And when his own life hung in the balance between heaven and earth, Jesus called out, "Father, I entrust my spirit into your hands!" (Luke 23:46).

On the surface, consistently doing the will of the Father sounds impossible. And it is, if we think of it in human terms. But when Jesus left earth for heaven, he sent his Spirit who enables us to know, to desire, and to do what pleases God. Of course, we're not perfect, so we make mistakes, but we're tracking for perfection. When we choose to do something that reflects God's heart, he promises we'll grow. And with growth, comes strength.

Strength, however, is not synonymous with wisdom. That's why we need to watch for and listen to God. When we observe him in creation and hear him in his Word, his direction for our lives becomes much clearer. Our weariness evaporates when we apply what God says to our difficult situations. His direction always leads us away from disintegration and toward renewal.

Finding God's direction and seeing things through his perspective improves the quality of our lives. When my vision started to deteriorate, I was reluctant to get glasses, but when I finally did, I couldn't believe how much easier they made my life. I could read without straining my eyes (or my arms as I had to hold the newspaper far away to read it). But more than that, my glasses freed me from the frustration of wanting to see clearly but not being able to. That's what happens when God's perspective becomes ours: It's much easier to see what's really going on in the world around us and in our lives.

Seeing things God's way protects us from ignorance and anxiety. We can trust him to take care of everything that's important to us: our spouses, children, homes, jobs. Like Jesus, we can give our Father those things, knowing he is capable of caring for them in the best way possible. Thankfully, we don't have to carry our burdens alone.

Jesus found relief from his burdens and rest and renewal in his Father's nourishment, direction, perspective, assurance, and preservation. The remedy for our weariness—true rest for our souls—is no different: we have to look to God for those same things in our lives. But we need humility to come to him. We have to be willing to say we're inclined to depend on other things and ourselves for renewal, that we don't completely agree that he alone is the source of life itself.

I often turn to other things for quick shots of energy or a sense of well-being. Without even thinking, I handle my weariness with caffeine, sugar, or by just pushing myself on. These are innocent solutions in themselves, but they remind me that at times I depend on my own quick fixes rather than finding rest in God.

My "get back to God" plan fell into that category. I relied on my own efforts to overcome my circumstances rather than depending on God to preserve me in them. Relying on God's preservation was only possible after I discovered that I was incapable of preserving myself.

We might read every book on fitness, take every vitamin known to humankind, use exercise equipment, practice yoga, jog, jiggle, and juice. But unlike body-level problems that can be solved with a body-level fix, weariness requires a soul-deep solution. Only God can infuse us with life and give us what we need to press on.

That night in my laundry room I rested my head in my hands and then looked at the floor. Slivers of moonlight slid slowly across my slippers. I tried to catch the slivers but they were too playful and slipped through my fingers.

Warmed by the moon's glow, I thought about Jim and the boys and how blessed I was to have a wonderful family. I reflected on my job and how much easier I had it than women who work full-time or raise their families by themselves. And because it was Christmas, I thought about Jesus who came to earth to die for my sins so I wouldn't have to. "Thank you for caring for me, Father," I whispered softly.

For the first time in a long while, God touched my soul with true rest. I saw how perfectly he had been caring for me all along. In working so hard to find him, I'd lost sight of him and his ability to sustain me. Nothing on my "get back to God" list was wrong, but as the moonbeams faded from the floor, I realized that God's ultimate gift to me was ultimate rest from the ultimate burden—sin.

No one knows what God has for us in the future, but as our Preserver, we do know what he has for us today. He provides strength to endure whatever he allows, his presence and Word to guide us through hard times, and his promise as we humble ourselves in our weariness: "Come to me, all of you who are weary and carry heavy burdens, and I will give you rest" (Matt. 11:28).

AND THERE HE WAS . . .

by Linda Toft

During a difficult time several years ago, I had to fly home to Virginia for family reasons. Even before I left, weariness and depression pressed in. I felt as if life's burdens were weighing me down—marriage, finances, kids. I'd packed my Bible in my suitcase so I'd have it while I was gone. But when I checked my luggage at the airport ticket counter, it was two pounds overweight. I decided to put my Bible in my carry-on bag instead.

During a layover en route, I opened my Bible in search of comfort and hope. I just didn't have the strength to go on. Psalm 23 led me to this passage in Isaiah:

> But now, O Israel, the LORD who created you says: "Do not be afraid, for I have ransomed you. I have called you by name; you are mine. When you go through deep waters and great trouble, I will be with you. When you go through rivers of difficulty, you will not drown! When you walk through the fire of oppression, you will not be burned up; the flames will not consume you" (Isa. 43:1, 2).

As I read these words, I saw that nothing could happen to me that God did not allow. I belonged to him and he knew me by name. He would always sustain and preserve me because he loved me. When I arrived in Virginia, I felt like a new person. My depression had lifted, and I was filled with joy, knowing I could rest in God's love.

Not long ago, I found myself in that familiar place again. I received a dreaded phone call from my sister: "Linda, Mom died. It happened this afternoon when she was sleeping." Grief nearly overwhelmed me in that moment.

The next week, I leaned more and more on God to hold me close in the midst of my deep sorrow and pain. And he did. Through the kindness of others and his Word, he sustained me through more than I ever thought I could bear. I still grieve, but I no longer fear I won't make it. I can trust him to be faithful and keep me no matter what.

4

GOD AS PROVIDER
Finding God in Our Needs

"If you only knew the gift God has for you and who I am,
you would ask me, and I would give you living water."
JOHN 4:10

 NEEDINESS. RESTLESSNESS. Discontent. A vague feeling that something is missing—missing from ourselves, our homes, our marriages, our bank accounts, our jobs, our lives. The belief that we lack something we deserve or that we have something we don't deserve at all, like illness or conflict. A restlessness that drives us to the hairstylist, the mall, the television, or the refrigerator for relief. There is a brief sense of satisfaction from our hairdo, a sitcom, a snack, or a sale item. Then the inevitable slide back to restlessness and discontent. It's what contemporary musician kd lang calls "constant craving."

We know the feeling well. Though sometimes we shrink from admitting it, especially when we should be grateful for all we have, we constantly hunger for something new, something different, something more. Our thoughts revolve around what to eat, buy, wear or where to go next. How to look younger, act older, or weigh less than we do. "If I could just paint the dining room, get a new bedspread, send my kids to the right college, have grandchildren, then I'd be satisfied. I'd be content." Kd lang was right about our constant craving; we're always wanting "more or other" but not for the reason we might think.

As strange as it may sound, we're constantly craving because God made us that way. He placed within us a longing for things we don't have so we would ask him to fill us and then give him thanks for providing the things we need. In fact, all need in our lives is actually the backdrop he designed against which to display his desire to be our Provider. He created us to depend on him for everything.

Our desire to feel satisfied is evidence of God's creative involvement in the universe and our lives. It's normal to sense lack and know something needs to be done about it. Whether it's physical, emotional, or spiritual, our ability to perceive neediness and our desire to assuage it is an integral part of our makeup that reflects God's lordship over us and creation.

The word *lord* has as its origin the meaning of "loaf bearer." It is accompanied by the idea of benevolence. The people of a land trusted the kindness of their lord to provide for them, and he would. God is our benevolent Loaf Bearer. We can trust in his kindness to supply us with everything we need, even when we don't know what we need or why we need it.

The problem is we don't want God to meet our needs—
we want to meet them ourselves. Like everything else it
touches, sin has corrupted the part of us that was made to
be satisfied by God alone. As a result, we've taken on the job
of "chief need-meeter," and we decide what we need and
when we need it. Unfortunately, we weren't designed or
equipped to do either. We don't know what we really need,
and the things we think will satisfy us don't. That's why we
move from place to place, thing to thing, person to person
in search of true contentment. Even creation groans under
the heavy weight of sin's effects in the world (which is waiting for everything to be reintegrated). God is restoring all
things through Christ, but until sin is abolished completely,
our longing for true contentment will remain.

A sign in front of a small country church says, "Contentment isn't having what you want. It's wanting what you
have." The only reason we ever want what we have is because
it satisfies us, it gives us that feeling of fullness. The minute
we lose that full feeling, we toss the thing or the experience
or the person aside and go after another. We keep that one
for a while, but the same thing happens again and again: we
lose the full feeling, and the cycle starts all over.

While resting by a well in Samaria, Jesus seized an opportunity to explain all of this to a woman in search of lasting
satisfaction.

> Jacob's well was there; and Jesus, tired from the long walk,
> sat wearily beside the well about noontime. Soon a
> Samaritan woman came to draw water, and Jesus said to
> her, "Please give me a drink." . . .

The woman was surprised, for Jews refuse to have anything to do with Samaritans. She said to Jesus, "You are a Jew, and I am a Samaritan woman. Why are you asking me for a drink?"

Jesus replied, "If you only knew the gift God has for you and who I am, you would ask me, and I would give you living water."

"But sir, you don't have a rope or a bucket," she said, "and this is a very deep well. Where would you get this living water?" . . .

Jesus replied, "People soon become thirsty again after drinking this water. But the water I give them takes away thirst altogether. It becomes a perpetual spring within them, giving them eternal life" (John 4:6, 7, 9–11, 13, 14).

In ancient times, *living water* described spring water because it bubbled up from the ground as if it were alive. Jesus wasn't telling the woman about a nearby active spring. He made the distinction between earthly and spiritual provisions and pointed to himself as the source of spiritual water that completely quenches spiritual thirst and gives eternal life.

In his letter to the members of the Philippian church, Paul assures them that God indeed provides us with everything we need from the riches given to us in Christ (see Phil. 4:19). God does not hold back any good thing from his children.

Like the woman at the well, we constantly crave but rarely understand what we really need. We're unaware or we forget that earthly things are temporary; their value and effect fades, leaving us empty and longing to be filled again. God's provisions for us are fundamentally different; their value and effect are eternal. He knows what we need and gives us what satisfies.

The Samaritan woman depended on earthly things to fulfill her. Some of us depend on relationships or money, others on success. I depend on beauty and order. When our family built a wooden walkway down a hill in our backyard to the beach for our son James's wedding, I was obsessed with the way I thought it should look. I thought, *Having a perfect walkway is part of having a perfect wedding. And I want the wedding in our backyard to be perfect.* When things in my world line up with my idea of beauty and order, I feel satisfied. Content. Not restless. When they don't, I'm either running around straightening pictures, so to speak, or I'm thinking about doing it.

Even though the grade of hill presented engineering challenges, I wanted the walkway even, level, and precise. Everyone involved did a masterful job of designing the walkway. They framed it just right, added risers for stairs, even used stainless-steel screws instead of nails that would rust. They worked in the heat, the rain, and swarms of bugs to make sure the walkway would be finished in time. Things were looking really good until Jim screwed down the first section of decking boards; he didn't space them evenly.

I know it sounds terrible, but all I could see was that the walkway lacked tidy spaces between deck boards. I didn't see how nicely the structure hugged the irregular grade of the sand dune or how secure it felt when I stood on it. I was upset with the whole project and with Jim for not being more careful. I even considered telling him the entire walkway was ruined—all because I didn't find the beauty and order I craved. I was looking in the wrong place for it.

My need for things to be right in this world is God-given, but when I look to earthly things to fill my need, I don't experience beauty and order or any other blessing. Instead, I experience disorder and ugliness. I ended up hurting Jim's feelings that day, which resulted in us having words later that night. He had worked hard on the walkway, yet I was far from satisfied.

The Bible is filled with stories about what happens when we look to something other than God to satisfy our needs. Like the story of the Samaritan woman, another story occurred in the desert.

> When Moses failed to come back down the mountain right away, the people went to Aaron. "Look," they said, "make us some gods who can lead us." . . . All the people obeyed Aaron and brought him their gold earrings. Then Aaron took the gold, melted it down, and molded and tooled it into the shape of a calf. The people exclaimed, "O Israel, these are the gods who brought you out of Egypt!" (Ex. 32:1, 3, 4).

After God's amazing display of his power and ability to fulfill their need for freedom from their four-hundred-year stint as slaves in Egypt, Israel rejected God and turned to an idol for satisfaction. God not only had caused Pharaoh to release them from captivity, but he also led them across dry ground through the Red Sea. In the wilderness, he provided manna from heaven, water from a rock, a pillar of fire to guide them at night, and a column of smoke to lead them by day. But the Israelites lost sight of God as their true Provider and turned to a god of their own making for "more and other."

What Israel didn't understand and what we often fail to remember is that God's provisions are always the right ones, even when they don't seem like it. He knows better than we do what our real needs are, and what he provides always fits those needs perfectly at exactly the time we need them. Even when they're practical provisions like food or shelter, what he gives is timely and sufficient.

But what about those times when we still feel empty, when a gnawing inside us just won't stop? Three scenarios offer partial explanations.

First, we believe we're entitled to certain things, that life owes them to us. Second, we've confused need with want. We find it difficult to distinguish between feelings produced by real or perceived emptiness. Third, our emptiness may stem from being unwilling to accept no for an answer.

When our boys were little, Jim and I thought twice before taking them to a toy store. The lesson that we can't have everything we want is almost as painful to teach as it is to learn when the students are two and six years old.

While these situations vary in detail, they all have one thing in common: they reveal the absence of contentment. Israel's reaction to God's seemingly slow response was triggered by discontent. They felt entitled to something God wasn't giving them, his leadership right then. So they turned to an idol for satisfaction instead of waiting for God to provide them with his perfect instructions—the Ten Commandments.

Even though it's always best to wait on God's provision, it's not always easy, especially when waiting means suffering.

Lisa believed God had something better for her nine-year-old son, so she managed to hang on through his suffering and her own. Finally, the doctors told her she had a choice. She could accept the available kidney, which was within margins but not a perfect match for Steven, or wait a while longer to see if another organ could be located, one closer to ideal compatibility.

Steven's condition worsened, but his mother believed God could provide something better than "within the margins." The slightest hint of organ rejection could send Steven's already fragile condition spiraling into decline.

"God, please hurry," Lisa prayed. "Steven's already so weak, and I don't know how much longer he can hold on." Early the next morning, a hospital in the next town called with amazing news—a perfectly matched kidney for Steven had become available during the night. Lisa raced to the hospital where Steven was already being prepped for surgery. The procedure went according to plan. Today, Steven is a healthy and active twelve-year-old boy.

We don't know the future, but God does. Sometimes his provisions come quickly. Sometimes he waits to reveal them. Other times they never come at all. Or so we think.

Imagine what would happen if we immediately received everything we ever thought we needed. . . .

Jim hoped for a major promotion, but it never happened. Six months later the company was bought out, and the position we'd hoped for was eliminated. Another time we desperately needed relief from a difficult situation but received a deeper faith in God's ability to sustain us instead. God may meet our needs by telling us no. What we think we need and what we really need aren't necessarily the same, and only he knows the difference. Sometimes we receive no for an answer, in order to find God's provisions.

When I asked God to give Jim a clean pathology report, he said no. Instead, Jim was diagnosed with cancer. *But God, I argued, this can't be good for any of us. Cancer is ugly and people die from it. You've got to take it away!* Again, his answer was no. People told me that everything would be all right, that God would take care of us and give us everything we needed to get through our ordeal, regardless of its outcome. But I remained unconvinced.

It took a long time and a lot of anger at God before I saw even the slightest hint of blessing in our circumstances. It happened on my way to visit Jim in the hospital one morning. *As bad as this is, it could be worse,* I found myself thinking. I'd gotten to know some of the other cancer patients on Jim's floor and their families. Several were already talking to hospice.

That realization was only the beginning. God continued to show me all the ways in which he was providing exactly what we needed: an expert team of doctors, places for James and John to stay when Jim went through rough spells at home, friends who brought food and stayed to pray, and a stripping away of much self-sufficiency and pride I never knew I had. The shocking thing now is that Jim and I would be willing to go through those gut-wrenching days all over again if it meant experiencing God's loving care and provisions the way we did and continue to do.

Once we realize how excellent God's provisions are, we'll prefer them to any others. At the same time, the Holy

Spirit enables us to recognize and wait for what our heavenly Father has for us when we're tempted to settle for less, to take the easy way out and grab snack food instead of waiting for a gourmet meal. Jesus dealt with a similar misunderstanding with his disciples when he asked, "You fathers—if your children ask for a fish, do you give them a snake instead? Or if they ask for an egg, do you give them a scorpion? Of course not! If you sinful people know how to give good gifts to your children, how much more will your heavenly Father give the Holy Spirit to those who ask him" (Luke 11:11–13).

The things we think fulfill us—relationships, reputations, traditions, possessions, knowledge—aren't bad things, but they were never meant to satisfy us in the ultimate sense. If we look to them instead of to God to give us what we crave—security, compassion, mercy, acceptance, and love—we can expect only temporary relief at best.

As humans we will always feel lots of wants and needs, from the trivial, "I really need a haircut" to the complex, "Boy, do I need that raise"—but what we really crave is wholeness in a world that's being repaired through Christ. This assures us that we're created in our Father's image. We find it easier to remember the difference between our supposed needs for money, or things, or perfectly spaced deck boards from our deepest, truest needs. We eagerly wait for the day when everything is right and complete. Most importantly, we simply keep our hands and hearts open for everything our Provider gives us, knowing that his provisions lead to lasting contentment and life itself.

AND THERE HE WAS . . .

by Betty Selig

I was living the American dream. I had a loving husband, two beautiful and healthy little girls, a third baby on the way, and a large, custom-built home in a lovely Pennsylvania suburb. I had it all, and it looked and felt wonderful. So what was the problem?

Things looked good on the outside but were slowly eroding on the inside. My husband's construction business was floundering. Rich and I had enjoyed years of prosperity—new vehicles, a yard full of toys for the kids, a custom-designed kitchen with my husband's hand-set tiles on the floor, walls, and counter backsplash. Suddenly, we didn't have enough money to pay our bills and bill collectors were calling.

The stress between my husband and me was building. We were both so worried that when we talked at all, our conversations often ended with one of us in tears and the other stalking out of the room.

The construction boom in our area seemed to be coming to an end, and Rich had trouble getting work. As his worry increased, his patience decreased. He felt he was working harder and harder but had to keep cutting his rates in order to keep busy. He worked more hours and made less money when he was able to work at all.

I felt helpless. I wanted to contribute financially but couldn't juggle work, home, and caring for two preschoolers. It hurt to see my hard-working husband so frustrated at not being able to provide for our family. Our stress went up another notch when our son was born. We wanted another child, but a new baby can turn up the heat in life.

For nearly a year, things at home grew steadily worse; work and income dwindled by the day. I felt stressed, pressured, and fearful about the future. This was a situation I had never encountered before; I'd always had what I needed to stand on my own two feet. Since talking to Rich only worried him, I kept my thoughts and emotions to myself and felt more and more isolated.

We were barely making ends meet and eating a lot of macaroni and cheese. I looked for part-time work, cut back on expenses, and shopped at secondhand stores and discount markets to make what little money we had go further. But it wasn't working.

While waiting with my daughter at her bus stop one morning, my friend Cathy noticed my distress. With tears rolling down my cheeks, I told her about our dire situation. She asked if she could pray for me. As she did, I felt strange but oddly comforted at the same time. Then she invited my family to church.

The next Sunday, we all went. The sermon was about Jesus and the disciples in a boat during a storm. The pastor seemed to describe our lives, for we felt as if we were being tossed all around and sinking fast.

Several weeks later, my husband and I accepted Christ as our Savior at Cathy's church. Soon after, God showed us that we needed to change the focus of our lives from what we wanted to what God wanted. Sometimes the process was slow and painful as we waited for God to lead us through each new crisis. We learned to stop and pray, then try to discern what pleased him instead of acting on our own impulses.

One day in prayer, God showed me that everything we had truly belonged to him, that he was the owner of it all. As such, he was free to do anything with it, even burn it up if doing so would bring him glory and us good. From that moment on, I knew we had to sell our house and get out of debt.

Selling our dream home was an agonizing decision. Our house reflected who we were and what we had achieved, but we were compelled to put a "For Sale" sign in our front yard.

While we waited for our house to sell, things got tougher financially. We weren't sure how we were even going to buy food. But somehow we knew God would meet our needs. And he did.

Several times we found bags of groceries on our front porch, in our car, or delivered by someone from church whom we barely knew. Occasionally, money arrived in the mail, sometimes with a signed note, other times anonymously. My parents and the leaders of our church were extremely generous and helpful. We wept tears of joy as we watched God use his people to care for us. Even though nothing in our circumstances changed, we believed that we would have a happy ending to our crisis.

Finally, our house sold for less than it had cost us, but we paid our debts, deposited a small amount in the bank, and moved into a rental unit. Amazingly, I felt God's peace in all of this. We now live in a small, modest home, and I'm no longer afraid to answer the phone. God has provided for us in ways that I would never have dreamed of.

During those days, we grew in our dependence on the Lord. Over and over, he demonstrated his faithfulness. He replaced our fears with confidence in him and our worries with the conviction that he could meet our needs. We learned about the dangers of holding on to earthly things too tightly. It's okay to enjoy what God gives, but we mustn't think they define us.

Rich and I have learned that God uses trials to teach us to depend on him completely and that our obedience to him is more important than possessions, positions, or power. Everything around us is temporary, so we need to invest our talents and energy into what will last for eternity.

It's not always easy, but I'm learning to live in deeper dependence on God. As I do, he gives me inner peace and joy that doesn't depend on circumstances. I'm seeing the importance of investing in the things God says are of value: relationships with others and with himself. These are eternal treasures that can't be lost or destroyed. And they are worth more than the American dream.

5

GOD AS DEFENDER
Finding God in Our Battles

"The Lord of hosts will defend them. . . . [He] will save
them in that day as the flock of His people; for they are
as the stones of a crown, sparkling in His land."
ZECHARIAH 9:15, 16 (NASB)

 WHEN JIM CALLED ME from the office at noon that day and asked, "Are you sitting down?" I knew. We'd been married for ten years, and he'd broken the news to me the same way every time. Always over the phone. Always with apprehension in his voice. And for ten years, my reaction had always been the same. With tears in my eyes and a knot in my stomach, I'd ask, "Where are we going, and when do we have to be there?"

Jim rattled off details about pack-up schedules and departure dates, but I never heard him. The minute he said, "I've got orders. We're going to Saudi Arabia," I stopped listening.

The U.S. Air Force was Jim's passion, and he was good at what he did in it. Though he was still a junior officer, he had the respect of colleagues many years his senior. But once again his dreams of a shining military career were moving to the forefront of our lives, and that meant that the thing most important to me was moving to the rear.

I wasn't interested in living overseas, especially since John, our second son, had just been born. I felt we should be close to our families, for my parents and Jim's mother to be a part of our children's lives. For at least a year, I secretly hoped that Jim would leave the service before accepting another assignment. Each new tour meant an additional commitment of up to three years. He'd always talked about going back to teaching high school someday. *Why not now?* I wondered.

When I married Jim, I knew all about the military lifestyle, having been raised in an Air Force family. As a youngster, I liked to move. It meant playing in boxes, exploring new neighborhoods with my brother Chip, and spying on people we didn't know yet. Whatever fears or anxieties I had, my mother's positive outlook put them to rest. She used to tell us, "Moving is fun! Moving is an adventure!"

When I was little, Mom was right. But when I became a teenager, things changed. Moving wasn't fun anymore. It hurt deeply to say good-bye to friends. By the time I entered my ninth school at age thirteen, I decided that having friends wasn't worth the pain I felt when I had to leave them behind.

I learned to cope with social challenges by shutting myself off from people, but internally I struggled with feelings of being exposed to danger. Not knowing my way around, making mistakes in public, being emotionally broadsided by news of having to move again, never feeling like I belonged anywhere. These became enemies over which Mom's approach to surviving upheaval no longer had power.

Now as an adult, the thought of relocating to the other side of the world was too much. I prayed Jim would reconsider his assignment to Saudi, but he wouldn't. In the days that followed his phone call, I felt as if I were at war.

I fought against Jim and his decision to press on with the overseas' move. I fought against the all-too-familiar sadness of having to tell friends "so long." I fought against our homeless, rootless existence. But most of all, I fought against my need to "buck up" and employ Mom's fun-loving and adventuresome outlook on moving. I wanted to, but this time I just couldn't.

I've got to make Jim understand how I feel so he'll change his mind, I kept telling myself. *I'm so tired of fighting with this lifestyle. I hate the instability. I want the moving to end.*

Tension mounted between Jim and me. Every time we talked about the impending move, we ended up arguing. I wanted to settle down. He wanted to serve his country. I knew from firsthand experience how hard the future could be for our boys; I attended thirteen schools in eleven years. He grew up in one place and wanted to see the world and thought our boys would, too. As the deadline to accept or reject his assignment drew closer, Jim and I grew farther apart.

"One more tour, and then I'll think about leaving the service," he finally said.

I replied, "I'm not sure I'll still be here."

I couldn't believe the words coming out of my mouth. For the first time in our marriage, someone alluded to divorce, and it was me. Feelings of insecurity had pushed me past the simple need for a stable home and threatened the one place left in my life where I felt I could seek shelter, safety, and protection—my marriage. Now it, too, was a dangerously unstable place. My heart broke. There was no simple way to fix the problem.

I wanted to smash something . . . break something . . . burst out of the trap I felt I was in. I hated Jim for not changing his mind about Saudi Arabia. I hated myself for not being able to conquer my emotions. And yes, I even hated God, who was ultimately responsible for the whole thing. I didn't turn to him for help. Instead, when I couldn't take it anymore, I did the only thing that made sense to me in the heat of the battle. I gave Jim an ultimatum: the Air Force or me.

I can still see him standing on our wooden deck, staring off into space. He looked like the weight of the world rested on his shoulders as he wrestled with his decision. Because of his military performance, it was no surprise that well-meaning, higher-ranking officers encouraged him to stay in the Air Force. But Jim's loyalty to our marriage eventually won out over their advice and his own professional goals—Jim withdrew his name from the eligibility list for overseas assignments. Shortly after, he submitted his military separation papers. Finally, the battle was over. Or was it?

Jim and I were both deeply wounded as we struggled to get on with our lives. He went from one interview to the next in search of a new job while he wrapped up ten years at his old one. I busied myself with the kids. Mostly, he and I kept our distance. The temptation to blame each other for our pain was great.

Two months later, it was mid-January, late in the day. I curled up in my chair in our living room. I'd gone there before to pray. For some reason, it was the place in our house where God seemed close by. Jim was gone. James was riding his bike. Inside, John was crying instead of napping in his crib, but I couldn't go to him—I was so tired of fighting. I just sat in my chair thinking and watching the afternoon shadows creep across the carpet.

My battle for stability had damaged our marriage. I was cold toward Jim—empty of desire for him—and I knew he felt the same way toward me. I'd finally won everything I thought I needed to feel secure, but I felt more vulnerable than ever before. "What's wrong with me? Why can't I feel safe?" Tears rolled slowly down my cheeks.

I slid out of my chair and onto the carpet where I lay facedown in the day's last strands of sunlight that spilled through the glass front door. Their warmth on my back felt like a hand gently resting on me, protecting me from the onslaught of doubt and confusion I faced. Then, feeling strangely reassured, I asked, "God, is that you?"

I didn't move. For twenty, maybe thirty minutes I stayed on the floor. "Oh God, if you're here, please don't leave me. I'm afraid."

Lying on the carpet in God's presence that afternoon, my heart ached for healing in my marriage. But at the same time, I wondered how Jim and I could ever feel safe with each other again after our sojourn through betrayal. What would it take to stabilize our marriage—confession, forgiveness, humility, faith, vulnerability? I was terrified of everything on the list. I wanted nothing more than to run away.

During that time, I began to think of the Christian journey as a difficult climb up a steep mountain. I didn't know it at first, but God's promises are the handholds and footholds we grab on to as he calls us out of the pits of our battles—our differences, our conflicts, and our despair.

Step by tentative step, we climb through the narrow pass cut into the side of the craggy, cold mountain called "Victory," sometimes with bloody hands from gripping God's promises so tightly. Those promises assure us that he places our feet where they need to be: a little to the left for praise, now back up a little for worship. And they fill our hearts with courage, knowing the God of the universe climbs beside us to shelter us from the things that try to push us down. In the end, God's promises make us like surefooted mountain deer that see the ascent as their way of life rather than something threatening.

My battle focused on my feelings of being lost and searching for my true home. For you, the conflict may be over money, kids, or jobs. It may put you at odds with your spouse or partner. In the end, the details don't really matter. What we think we're fighting against is never the real issue. Instead, the real fight is within our own souls where we battle to believe that God defends us against our adversaries, whether they are circumstances, other people, or ourselves.

Like a good shepherd, God's defense includes leading us through dark places to get us to safety. "Even when I walk through the dark valley of death, I will not be afraid, for you are close beside me. Your rod and your staff protect and comfort me" (Ps. 23:4). When we pass through hard and painful places, we don't have to fear for we are not alone. God's knowledge, power, and presence go before us and surround us. Every step we take is under the watchful care of one who loves us, protects us, and brings us back to the course if we stray. We are valuable and precious to God. He will neither leave us nor forsake us (Heb. 13:5). No one can steal us out of his hand (John 10:28, 29). If our Defender is for us, who can possibly be against us? (Rom. 8:31).

It would be much easier if we instinctively believed God will defend us, but we don't. So he orchestrates our lives to show us the unreliability of the things upon which we rely for our defense instead of him. The stock market takes a dive. A child becomes ill. Our spouse is transferred, our marriage unravels.

Nowhere in Scripture or in life do we see that it's easy to believe that God defends us. It isn't. Like learning to walk, it's scary at first. We're so used to holding onto other things for security that we find it difficult to let go of them and trust God to protect us instead.

When we trust God as our defense, we can embrace life with passion. We no longer try to make the present be what the past wasn't in order to be safe in the future. We let go of our self-sufficiency and self-interpretation of circumstances and rely instead on God to shield us from undue suffering.

Trusting him to defend us means freedom from fear, anxiety, and doubt. We find then that the journey is not too hard for us to complete, that God's way of getting where we need to be is not beyond our reach.

So how do we trust God to defend us? As I slowly learned, we let go of our earthly defenses. Instead of clinging to them in dark, scary places, we listen for God to whisper to our hearts, "Fear not, for I am with you." We rejoice with the psalmist, who declared, "I love you, LORD; you are my strength. The LORD is my rock, my fortress, and my savior; my God is my rock, in whom I find protection. He is my shield, the strength of my salvation, and my stronghold" (Ps. 18:1, 2). When we remember who God is, we take the first step in remembering what he does for us.

Finding God as Defender enables us to live in joyous abandon because we believe the truth. If your parents hurried to you when you cried out in your sleep from a bad dream, you experienced the power of their presence. It soothed and comforted you, then enabled you to drift back to sleep—to reenter the very place that once frightened you.

That's how it is with God. When we cry out to him, he comes because he loves us. Not only does he "check under the bed for monsters" in the moment, but he also stays with us, assuring us it's okay to be wherever he's called us.

For years, I believed that if I could settle down someplace once and for all, my insecurities would vanish. I could rest in my relationships, knowing they weren't going to go away. I could let my hair down, be real with people, and be at home. I looked to an environment to protect me from feeling insecure and vulnerable because I didn't know that God alone is my rock, my fortress, and my stronghold. I didn't realize he always defends what belongs to him, including marriage.

The climb wasn't easy. A cold wind blew through my heart for a long time. At first, my legs were weak, and it didn't take much to knock me off balance. But God strengthened me every time I remembered that he is stable, dependable, and solid. He gave me confidence to step out into the impossible.

God defends his people with his promises. Jim and I are proof of that. We're still together and very much in love. It's been fifteen years since the possible move to Saudi Arabia. We've finally settled in Florida, the home of my dreams, but through no plan of ours. God used Jim's bout with cancer to bring us to our home near the beach.

I look at the palms of my hands every now and then, half expecting to see scars from holding onto God's promises so tightly. But instead of scars, I see the beginning of calluses. I hear they come the longer we climb.

If you look at your own hands, you'll probably see calluses, too. They'll look a little like trust, a little like courage. But mostly they'll look like love that always defends you and never lets you go. No matter how high the climb is or how frightened you are, God faithfully defends you all the way to the top.

AND THERE HE WAS . . .

by Patti Sapp

"**I** hate you!" Matt yelled at me on a regular basis. As his first-grade teacher, I cared deeply for him, but his abusive outbursts were hard to take. I felt ill equipped to face him each morning, so I searched the Bible for guidance on how to handle the fiery six-year-old and took Paul's advice to "keep on praying" (1 Thess. 5:17).

I asked God to defend my place in Matthew's life. He needed special attention, and I wanted to give it to him. But Matt's disruptive behavior was hard on everyone, not just me. So I asked God to restrain Matt whenever parent volunteers and the principal were nearby and to protect the other children in my classroom. But the outbursts continued.

During one memorable episode, Matt threw a chair in class. It narrowly missed little Emily, who jumped behind me for protection. I stood there, stunned. Then, while yelling at the top of his lungs that he hated me, Matthew bolted for the classroom door only to miss and crash into me instead. Startled, he looked up and blurted, "Did you know my mom's gonna get fired because of the change?"

I was confused by his comment, but I focused on my own anger and frustration: "Why aren't you helping me, Lord? Where is your defense? Why did I end up with this child in my classroom?" I asked God. "Why won't you answer my prayers?"

After the chair-throwing incident, I needed to call Matt's mother to discuss his behavior. And I wanted her to clarify his odd comment about "change." When I reached his mom, she told me that her job as a high school cafeteria worker was in jeopardy. She couldn't make correct change at the cash register and endured constant ridicule and complaints from the students. Since her boss had warned her several times, she was convinced that the next one would result in her losing her job.

Matt's mother also described her difficult home life with her children. She barely provided their basic necessities, much less the attention they all craved. She was in a state of despair. I offered to help her practice her money-changing skills, but I wasn't sure how that was going to help Matthew.

When the phone call to Matt's mom was over, I broke down in tears as I saw his situation more clearly. I pleaded with God to rescue him and agreed to be obedient if his plan involved me. But how could it? Then I remembered a passage from the book of Proverbs: "Trust in the LORD with all your heart and lean not on your own understanding; in all your ways acknowledge him, and he will make your paths straight" (Prov. 3:6 NIV). In that moment, God gave me a sense of his peace and protection even though the turmoil in my classroom continued.

I was excited when Matt's mom decided to let me tutor her. Our sessions began shortly after our phone conversation. Several afternoons a week, she and I sat at a small table in my classroom and worked in identifying the value of each coin while Matt played with puzzles and games. In the beginning, I wasn't sure how I'd fit our sessions into my already full schedule, but God stretched my time and gave me patience as he used me to fulfill his purpose in the little boy's life and family.

Over time, Matthew inched his way closer to the table where his mother and I practiced how to make and give change. Slowly, his icy attitude toward me began to thaw. The difference was slight at first, but I could feel him warming up to me. I'll never forget the afternoon I caught Matt smiling at me for the first time. He had adorable dimples!

Matt's mom quickly progressed in our tutoring sessions. I suggested role-playing activities, and encouraged Matt to play along by pretending to purchase food from her. We all joked and laughed. It warmed my heart to see Matt and his mom working and playing together.

Our afternoon sessions continued for several more weeks. I was amazed at the changes in Matt's behavior in my classroom. His outbursts became less frequent, and he spoke rather than yelled during class time. The other children included him in conversations and games. In short, Matthew was blossoming into a pleasant, well-liked little boy.

God's path for Matthew and his mom hadn't been easy for any of us. In fact, at times I wondered if we'd all make it. But we did. I found that I needed to cling to God's promise to direct me as I trusted him when the going got rough.

The transition from frustration to peace was gradual in Matt's family, but God's presence was clear: Matt's mom kept her job and Matt's behavior improved.

And I experienced the power of God's defense. God provided extra energy, day-care arrangements for my own young children, and the sense of gratification I experienced while helping Matt and his mom. I simply obeyed.

But the sweetest evidence of God's defense through hard times came late one afternoon after school. While straightening my desk, I ran across a crumpled-up piece of paper. I smoothed out the wrinkles and instantly recognized Matt's handwriting. It read, "Do you know that I love you now?"

6

GOD AS TEACHER
Finding God in Our Confusion

"The LORD, your Redeemer, the Holy One of Israel, says:
I am the LORD your God, who teaches you what is good
and leads you along the paths you should follow."
ISAIAH 48:17

 JIM AND I sat next to each other in the examining room and held hands. After three months, his cancer treatments were finally over. He was weak from daily doses of radiation and seven hard rounds of chemo, but we were grateful he was alive.

When Jim was diagnosed with cancer, everything was a rush. We couldn't slow down to process what was happening to us. We just reacted and kept on reacting until the initial crisis was over. Throughout his grueling course of treatment, things moved almost as quickly. We barely handled everything we had to do. We had little or no time to think, reflect, or plan.

Finally, things were slowing down. Now it was time to hear about ongoing medical care: how often Jim would need to see the doctors, what type of scans were required to check for recurrences, when he could expect to get stronger and feel better. It was a meeting about coming out of sickness into at least provisional health. It was a meeting not about the problematic present but about the future, our future.

That's why Jim's question nearly took my breath away. Just before Dr. Morrow walked into the room, Jim turned to me and asked, "Where do we go from here?"

"What do you mean?" I asked.

He dropped his gaze to the floor. "You know what I mean," he sighed.

But I didn't.

Throughout our entire cancer experience, I was confident that when it was all over, we'd go back to living like we did before. Jim would work for his company, I'd write magazine articles, and the boys would fill our home with laughter again. It never occurred to me that things would be different, but how could they be the same when we had all changed so much?

Physically, Jim's body had been permanently altered. He'd lost a significant amount of weight during his treatments and was unable to regain it. The left side of his neck bore permanent scars of the surgery, leaving it smaller than the right side. The fifty near-lethal doses of radiation that destroyed any remaining tumor cells in Jim's throat had also destroyed his salivary glands. He couldn't talk, eat, or sleep without first replacing lost moisture in his mouth with a sip of water. All these physical changes had repercussions. Because eating was difficult, Jim no longer looked forward to meals. Going out for dinner now made him uncomfortable. The challenge of eating, a lack of endurance, and slow-healing radiation burns kept him from being like he used to be.

Jim's cancer also made an impact on us both emotionally. I felt angered when I thought of what we had been through and how much cancer had altered him. I felt impatient as I waited to get through the problems and back to normal. I felt guilt over my inability to accept my situation as heaven-sent. If I believed God was sovereign and could protect me from unnecessary suffering, why was I fighting against the way things were? And I felt mounting fear when I thought about my life as it was—fortysomething with two kids, an elusive future, and a husband I didn't know anymore.

Like a military veteran who suffers from post-traumatic stress long after the battle's end, I felt worse—not better—now that our fight against cancer seemed to be over. I felt disoriented by what was strange and what was familiar. If you've ever gone home after being away for a long time, you know what I mean: the absence of the big oak tree in the town square; a new subdivision of tract homes where acres of corn used to grow; a second story added to the old high school; or a new four-lane road to the airport. It's the same town all right; it's just not the same place. One finds it difficult if not impossible to accept the changes as meaningful, much less good. I was disoriented by the combination of what was different and familiar in him and unable to see beyond my longing for what he used to be.

Finally, by changing both him and me, cancer changed us as a couple. Fear of what might happen to him next, what might happen to both of us next gripped us. Would we have enough money to pay all the bills? Would Jim's company allow him to stay on despite his limited ability to work? We argued over the different ways we tried to cope with the whole situation. Jim shut down and backed away from me, while I reached out to him for reassurance and comfort. Honesty and intimacy were much harder to come by than I had expected.

In one way, our war was over: Jim had made it through his treatments. But we had to fight another battle—we had to survive Jim's survival.

In the weeks that followed that doctor's appointment, my emotions bounced all over the place. One minute I was overjoyed that Jim was alive. The next minute I could hardly look at him; he reminded me too much of suffering. One minute I was thrilled that his treatments were over; the next, a single moan or cough from him would send me spiraling into gut-wrenching fear that the treatments were not over, the enemy not vanquished after all. I had hoped for a future with Jim that I could hold on to. Yet now that that future was here, I was bewildered. I felt like a top spinning off balance, all wobbly and spastic. Life didn't make sense anymore, and I was confused.

Confusion comes at us from a multitude of places. For me I couldn't find my familiar husband in the new husband that life had given me. For some, confusion might come from an unexpected turn in a child's behavior, a career change, or in faltering health. Regardless of the source of our particular and personal confusion, we need to remember that God's teaching is always the solution to it.

When we find ourselves lost, confused, disoriented, we need only recognize God as our Teacher in order to benefit from his loving instruction. Sometimes that's an easy thing to do; sometimes it's not. Our own vision of how things should be often makes it difficult to accept God's opportunities for soul-level growth. His way of teaching and why he teaches can look different from what we're used to.

In Isaiah's record, God's self-designation as the Holy One reminds us that he is pure and righteous. We can trust that all his ways are good and right. That includes his motives. We're not told that we must love painful experiences and the confusion they bring. Rather, we accept them on the basis of who God is, a good Teacher who loves us and will not allow us to be crushed by the things he uses to mold us into the image of his Son (see 2 Cor. 4:8–10).

Too often, we think we're the center of the universe, that everything is meant for us, even knowledge. But the truth is God is at the center of all things. That's why everything in creation exists. The heavens tell of his glory, and the skies display his magnificent craftsmanship. They speak of these things day after day, night after night without ceasing (see Ps. 19:1–4). Their reason for being is to make God known. In other words, they teach.

As his creatures, we're also designed to declare the glory of God. Our lives should show forth his goodness, kindness, holiness. Even our survival instinct is designed to reveal things about God. When we gather berries, when we guard the entrance to our "caves," and when we shelter our young, he shows us that he is our Provider—he gives us food; as our Defender—he gives us safety; and as our Creator—he gives us life. God wants to teach us about himself, and he uses life as his classroom.

More than any teaching the world offers, we benefit most from God's teaching. It dispels our questions. Which job should I take? Why is my marriage so hard? How can I help my friend who struggles with addiction? God imposes his orderly truth onto disorderly confusion. In fact, that's what confusion is—being mixed up. Jumbled together. Bewildered. Perplexed. Unable to distinguish what's what. Do you ever feel that way? As I've confided throughout this book, I certainly do. Thankfully, God's instruction untangles our confusion and illumines our thinking so we can move forward on his path for our lives.

Unlike a teacher tired or disinterested, God instructs us through life experiences, Scripture verses, parables and stories, and special people we meet. Some of his lessons are unexpected or even undesirable. We don't want to learn from cancer, from loss, from shame, but we do. Trials become opportunities for learning and blessing when we accept them as teaching tools in the hand of the Master Teacher. The apostle James describes the value of learning and growing through trials this way:

Dear brothers and sisters, whenever trouble comes your way, let it be an opportunity for joy. For when your faith is

tested, your endurance has a chance to grow. So let it grow,
for when your endurance is fully developed, you will be
strong in character and ready for anything (James 1:2–4).

Few of us rejoice when we get into tough places. In fact,
we can hardly wait to get out of them. In the beginning
stages of Jim's recovery, all I could think about was getting
back to our life the way it had been before. What I didn't
understand is that we can never go back to our past. We can't
recreate something that doesn't exist. Only God can do that.
When reality failed to yield my expectations, I was disoriented and confused since I couldn't go back to life before
cancer. However, my confusion has turned out to be fertile
soil in which God has planted a deeper understanding of his
loving sovereignty.

God uses changing circumstances to teach me that he has
ultimate authority over me and those circumstances. I need
to practice humble submission to his reign in my life and to
make choices. I can be sad over what no longer is or be thank-
ful for what remains, namely that Jim is alive and cancer free.
I can lament that we are not the same people we were, or I
can celebrate that we are stronger ones. I won't be surprised
if we find out in heaven that much of the trouble and anguish
we feel here on earth are actually *growing pains* in disguise.

Even beyond the forms in which he delivers his teachings,
God is the most generous of all instructors. He knows we
need all the help we can get. He doesn't teach in one voice or
manner. He offers many kinds of lessons and a whole range
of guidance. He exposes us to everything necessary for us to

get the point. He is willing to offer the bigger lessons in phases. God knows we can handle only so much at one time. He takes us through each level of life's experiences to teach us what we need to know about him, even when we don't think we're ready for it yet.

My friend Becky knows; she's been there. "I thought the doctor would never come back into the office with the test results," she confided to me one day. "Mark and I were suspicious because I'd been feeling like when I was pregnant, but we didn't want to get our hopes up. The thought of going through that cycle of hope and disappointment again was more than we could bear."

Becky and Mark had been married for seven years and had been trying to have a baby. No one could explain why she'd been unable to carry to term. At the age of twenty-eight, she'd already suffered three miscarriages and the searing heartache that went with each one.

"We really thought it would be different this time," she said that day. Tears ran down her cheeks. "But it wasn't. I miscarried shortly after that doctor's visit. We were devastated. Mark and I couldn't understand why the one thing we wanted most in life was apparently out of our reach."

As she later saw, God himself was leading Becky and her husband through difficult experiences. At the time, they couldn't fathom the reason for their pain. But shortly after Becky's last miscarriage, she met Caitlin, who was pregnant, unwed, and trying to decide whether or not to keep the baby. Her family wasn't supportive, and the baby's father was nowhere to be found.

During their first conversation, Becky shared her story with Caitlin. They met two more times to talk over coffee. A week later, Mark, Becky, and Caitlin saw an attorney to discuss adoption proceedings.

Only the day before they'd met, Caitlin asked God to show her what to do about her situation. If Becky had not been through the trials of miscarriage, she and Mark never would have considered adoption. Today, they have a precious little girl named Joy. God used layers of circumstances to teach Caitlin, Becky, and Mark about his faithfulness, mercy, and love.

God takes us beyond where we want to go to where we need to be spiritually. He's like a special teacher or educator who sees more in us than we see ourselves. This teacher stays late to help us with difficult assignments. He or she holds us accountable for doing our work and teaches us through example, not through lectures. But most importantly, this special teacher wants to see us grow. God does, too.

The apostle Peter encouraged fellow believers to crave spiritual food the way a baby cries for milk (see 1 Pet. 2:2, 3). Like milk, God's Word and his ways nourish us, making us strong and turning life into something more exciting than we ever dreamed possible. Whenever we feel challenged on our spiritual journeys with God, we need to remember it's only because he loves us too much to leave us behind.

When we feel confused, God takes us by the hand. He walks beside us in our pain instead of lecturing us. He leads by gentle example. To demonstrate humility, for instance, Jesus knelt down and washed his disciples' feet. "I have given you an example to follow. Do as I have done to you," he told them. When Peter refused to be washed by Jesus, the Lord told him, "You know these things—now do them! That is the path of blessing" (John 13:15, 17). Jesus leads us to the path of blessing by showing us where it is and how to get there.

When soldiers arrested Jesus in the garden later that night, Peter drew his sword and cut off the ear of the high priest's servant.

Jesus rebuked Peter. "Put your sword back into its sheath. Shall I not drink from the cup the Father has given me?" (John 18:10, 11).

Jesus had told Peter ahead of time that he was going to betray him. In shock and horror, Peter professed his undying loyalty to Jesus. But after Jesus' arrest, Peter denied him three times in order to save himself from suffering (see Luke 22:56–62).

Peter's story shows us God's resolution as a Teacher and his patience in action. He is willing to teach the same or a similar lesson time and again. He doesn't ridicule our dullness. He doesn't turn away when we don't understand. He doesn't flunk us out of class when we're slow. He hangs in there even when we turn away from him, rejecting his lessons or his love. We might temporarily lose sight of his presence, but we can't forfeit him as Teacher, no matter what we do.

At times we face specific choices or decisions, and we don't know what God wants us to do. How do we know if we should move aging parents in with us or into retirement facilities? How do we find God's direction for specific circumstances? Or his teaching in the choices he leads us to make?

As a rule, we can ask three questions in those situations, which might help us find our answers.

- First, do our options clearly violate God's Word in any way?

- Second, does one option bring peace or make us unsettled? There's an old saying: When in doubt, don't.

- Finally, what do our godly counselors recommend? Sometimes our direction comes from without, not from within.

Experiencing God as Teacher is not a matter of devoting more effort or finding more time. We need to remember that he is patiently teaching at all times, even in the midst of hard circumstances when his presence feels the furthest away. When we have faith that he is always teaching and when we expect to learn from him in all of our experiences, his guidance emerges in the right way and at the right time.

In the months since that meeting in the doctor's office, God's teaching has helped me reflect on Jim's quiet question: "Where do we go from here?"

I don't know where we are going, except that our future will not look like our past. God's teaching helped me relinquish my own vision of how my life will be. It has helped me accept that my confusion itself is a lesson, a reminder that he is working in my life.

I don't pretend that I've learned these lessons fully. I still catch myself thinking that God has gauged my situation incorrectly. And I still pray he will give me less difficult lessons through which to grow from here on!

But whatever any of your personal circumstances happen to be, recognizing God as Teacher offers not just knowledge and direction, but the comfort that his teaching is eternal. You don't have to work harder to benefit from his teaching, but you can relax knowing he's alongside you.

Above all, you can draw comfort from knowing that pain and bewilderment are places of learning, even when the lesson isn't clear. The outcomes God plans for you may not be what you expect, but they will always be what's right and will always teach you. Knowing this, you can embrace your confusion as a chance to hear God's voice and find a new way. Then you can consider your trials as opportunities to find joy. God will use them to teach you what is good and to lead you along the paths you should follow.

AND THERE HE WAS . . .

by Pastor Howard Alperin

When I was a young child, my parents told me that I was Jewish, and that was very special. They said we were Orthodox, which meant I had to wear a yarmulke (skull cap) and tzitzit (fringe on the corner of my garment). We attended an Orthodox synagogue occasionally, and my parents sent me to a Jewish school. But they removed me after I came home one day and told my mother that we needed to keep kosher and we could not go out to eat on Friday night (the Jewish Sabbath begins at sundown on Friday). Mother said we were not that Jewish.

I've always loved my family, but I was confused about my religious upbringing. Even though observing the Sabbath meant not driving, handling money, or using electricity, my mother lit the Sabbath candles at home and then we went to Shoney's Big Boy for dinner. My mother wouldn't cook or clean on the Sabbath, but she would go to all the Saturday sales. The only time we went to the synagogue was on the high holidays—Rosh Hashanah (Jewish New Year) and Yom Kippur (the Day of Atonement). I was confused and desperate for answers, but I didn't know where to find them.

When I was seventeen, I left home and trained as a paramedic. All through school and at work, I wondered where God was in the pain and suffering I saw every day.

I stopped attending the synagogue; my truancy lasted more than three years. During that time, I dated a nurse and went to church with her several times, but I didn't find God there. Shortly after, I met and fell in love with another nurse. I attended a few church services with her, too. But still no God. No girl either; we broke up because I wouldn't keep going to her church.

In the late '70s, I met a wonderful girl. We were married, and she became the mother of my two daughters. I went to church with her, believing God must be where she worshiped because the services were held on Saturday. But he wasn't there.

As the years went by, the pain from what I saw every day on my job and from not having a relationship with God increased. My marriage became disheveled, and I grew distant from my two young daughters. Still no God.

My grandfather, seeing my pain and futile search asked me to come back and honor my faith. I became Jewish again. For the next two years, I pursued Orthodox Judaism and attended yeshiva (rabbinical school) in New York City. I wore a black hat and suit as well as my yarmulke and tzitzit. I went to synagogue three times a day for prayer, and I studied ten hours daily except on the Sabbath and holidays. I learned the Torah's 613 commandments plus all the rabbinic laws in the Mishnah and Talmud. But still no God. After two years and more pain, I sold my Orthodox attire and returned home to Memphis where I resumed working as a paramedic.

I met Gloria in the early '90s. She was the most beautiful woman I'd ever seen. Soon after, we were married.

Gloria went to church. Even though she often invited me, I wasn't interested; I'd been to church before and hadn't found God there.

After a few years, Gloria asked me to go with her to see a Passion Play during an Easter service at her church, and I went. I was not interested until they scourged Jesus. With each lash of the Roman whips, I watched and listened. The words of the prophet Isaiah flooded my thoughts. Those lashes were meant for me.

By the time the play reached the crucifixion, tears ran down my cheeks. I sobbed as Isaiah 53:5 (NIV) ran through my mind: "He was pierced for our transgressions, he was crushed for our iniquities; the punishment that brought us peace was upon him, and by his wounds we are healed." Suddenly, God was there!

In that moment, I realized that God had always been there. I was the one who'd been distant. My heart felt full of joy, not pain and loneliness. I accepted Christ as my Redeemer, and he has been with me ever since.

God isn't far away. According to Hebrews 13:5, he never leaves us nor forsakes us. I've since attended the International Theological Seminary where I graduated with a degree in theology. I'm no longer a paramedic; I minister to the homeless and shut-ins. But I still see pain and loneliness in those I care for. It lifts my heart when I share God's love with them, and they realize they are not alone.

Today God continues to do miracles in my life. He is here indeed!

7

GOD AS KING
Finding God in Our Hearts

"I will praise you, my God and King,
and bless your name forever and ever."

PSALM 145:1

 I GREW UP BELIEVING that the world should be a happy place. Unhappiness, pain, anger, and fear were weaknesses or personal failures. I learned early on to deny such feelings and to avoid situations in which those feelings emerged. Even as a Christian, I avoided visiting someone in the hospital or helping someone in need. I grew adept at going through the motions of caring without ever going toe-to-toe with suffering.

When Jim's cancer came, my running from difficult circumstances was no longer an option. Even then, I tried desperately to dodge the pain. Some of my avoidance techniques were self-destructive, such as becoming overdependent on the antianxiety and sleeping medications that helped me cope. Other techniques, like my all-night movie marathons or end-less phone conversations with friends, were fairly innocent. And some may have even had a useful side to them, like spending hours reading mountains of information about alternative cancer treatments for Jim.

The problem with these strategies was that I turned away from where I really was. Behind them all was my con-viction that nothing worthwhile could come from being in the awful place I was in. It took me a long time to accept the idea that no matter what we encounter in our lives, we are living in the kingdom of God.

God's kingdom has always been at the center of Chris-tianity. Kingdom thought was the central aspect of Jewish theology and everyday life. The Old Testament was filled with teachings about it, and the Jews waited eagerly for it. Even the Roman government was familiar with it. When Jesus was a baby, Herod's order to murder all the male chil-dren in the region under the age of two was an attempt to derail any royal competition; Herod had heard rumors con-cerning the coming King of the Jews.

Today the kingdom of God—the sovereign and gracious expression of his will—has already come in the person of Jesus Christ, God's appointed King. His rule and reign were inaugurated during his earthly ministry (see Matt. 4:17). The fullness of his kingdom when all sin is abolished, wholeness exists on every level of life, and every knee bows before him and confesses him as King is still set for a future time (see Rev. 11:15). In a way, the Kingdom is already and not yet.

Just as earthly kingdoms reflect the nature of their earthly kings, the kingdom of God reflects the nature of its eternal King who is holy and separate from us. When this King of the universe pulled back the curtains of heaven for Isaiah to see him, this is what the prophet wrote down:

> In the year that King Uzziah died, I saw the LORD sitting on a throne, high and lifted up, and the train of His robe filled the temple. Above it stood seraphim; each one had six wings: with two he covered his face, with two he covered his feet, and with two he flew. And one cried to another and said: "Holy, holy, holy is the LORD of hosts; the whole earth is full of His glory!" And the posts of the door were shaken by the voice of him who cried out, and the house was filled with smoke. So I said: "Woe is me, for I am undone! . . . For my eyes have seen the King, the LORD of hosts" (Isa. 6:1–6 NKJV).

Isaiah saw God's majesty. We need to see it, too. So often, we lose sight of our King's regal splendor. Part of the reason may be that as Americans, we're far removed from royalty. When I was sixteen, I lived with my family in London for a year. England's strong sense of its royal heritage was reflected in nearly every aspect of life from advertising, to customs and traditions, to everyday colloquialisms. It was clear that their view of their monarchial history had shaped them as a nation. In a similar way, our understanding of God's holiness and majesty shapes our view of his kingdom and his role in it as our King.

God's holiness is the cornerstone of his kingdom. *Holy* means to be set apart, to be completely *other*. God is set apart and completely *other* from his creation that is stained by sin. God is untouched by sin, utterly clean. Even that which proceeds from him—his motives, his intentions, his love for us, his rule and reign in our lives—is pure. We have nothing to fear in the kingdom of God. We are safe and deeply loved. When God's holiness frames our thoughts of him as King, our hearts are far more likely to respond to his power and majesty with gratitude and praise.

The psalmist shouted praises to God when he saw his power and majesty through his works of creation (see Psalm 104). His authority, strength, and wisdom are visible in the things he has made. Have you ever stood at the seashore or walked a mountain trail and been overcome by the beauty all around you? That's your heart shouting praises to God. When you hold a newborn baby or watch the sun rise, the quiver you feel is your soul straining to worship.

God's majesty is also revealed in his law which he gives us to obey in the strength of his grace (see Ezek. 36:26, 27). Even though obedience to his commands doesn't come naturally, our King loves us enough to give us the means by which we can walk in them. As if that weren't enough, God rewards us with his comfort and *love tokens* to encourage us in holiness. Even when we make mistakes, he corrects us to sanctify us on our way to complete holiness in heaven. Imagine how hopeless we'd be without our King's kind help.

Just as our view of God is incomplete apart from his majesty, our view of him as King is incomplete apart from his grace. The essence of his grace is the cross. Through the cross, God's kingdom with all its blessings and benefits moves from heaven into our lives. But obviously that doesn't mean that living in the kingdom of God is always easy.

We find it difficult to live in God's kingdom because it's so different from anything we're used to. Nothing about kingdom living resembles the way of the world, which is where the King found us. The Kingdom involves God's people living in a fallen world with his power operating in their lives by his Spirit and through his Word.

The values, patterns, and outcomes in the Kingdom are opposite from the world's. What's up is down, and what's down is up. For example, the world says we gain life when we keep it for ourselves. God says we gain life when we give it to others. The world values success, power, and recognition. God values meekness, gentleness, and humility. A life lived for itself produces loneliness and brokenness. A life lived for God produces the fruit of his Spirit—love, joy, peace, patience, kindness, goodness, faithfulness, gentleness, and self-control (see Gal. 5:22, 23).

When I first arrived in England, I had no idea how many wonderful things I could see and do. The longer I lived there, I appreciated much of what it offered. I liked sipping hot tea and munching scones on cold, gray afternoons and listening to the locals carry on about politics and religion standing atop wooden crates on Speakers' Corner. It's the same way in the Kingdom. As time passes, we grow in our understanding and our appreciation for being here.

Many of us miss the comfort of living in the Kingdom because we forget the integrity of our King. In the world's kingdom, we're afraid, not able to trust others, not sure of love. Unlike his earthly counterparts, God's sovereign rule in our lives is just, right, and pure. He understands everything about us—our doubts, our pain. His decisions are always right from every angle, and his perspective is the standard for all others. God can't be bought, won't sell out, and is the essence of faithfulness. He is our friend. His kingdom is a safe place where nothing can destroy us. Even death's sting has been snuffed out. Our King is trustworthy. He cares for us and loves us because we are the *apple of his eye.*

Everything God does in his kingdom brings healing to our lives. Sometimes it happens almost without our notice. Other times, he works through obvious circumstances. Either way, we can't live kingdom life on the surface. We have to go deep because healing happens from the inside out.

Four months after Jim's cancer treatments ended, I sat in the same hospital waiting room. Once again I waited for the doctor to come out of the operating room with results of more biopsies; a posttreatment scan had revealed a suspicious spot in Jim's throat.

That morning I struggled with fear and anxiety. Everything in me was shaking. A friend was supposed to wait with me during Jim's surgery but became sick at the last minute. Except for two women on the other side of the waiting area, I sat alone.

To try to settle my feelings, I picked up a Bible from a small table by my chair. The only passage I could think of was my favorite section in Job: "Where were you . . . ?"

I thought back to the night on my patio when God used the stars to teach me something important about who he is: as Creator, he has everything under control. I didn't stop shaking completely, but I felt calmer inside and more willing to accept the fact that being where I was could be all right.

Jesus understood that fact when he chose to stay where his Father had put him. He didn't run from the cross and the suffering it required. Instead, he accepted his circumstances in order to accomplish his Father's will, knowing that good would come. Accepting hard things in our lives doesn't mean we have to like them. It means we allow them to operate in our lives to accomplish what God intends.

Seeing God as a king who maintains order in creation while loving it, made it okay to be in his kingdom that day. The pathology report on the biopsies came back negative, and I took Jim home a few hours later. I sat on the edge of our bed thinking while he dozed. *I guess trials really have no power of their own unless we think they do. God rules over them and releases them into our lives in just the right way for them to do exactly what they're supposed to do.*

To be honest, I'm still learning how to look at life that way. Even with what I know so far, I don't always remember how to think or act when I'm sideswiped by chaos, guilt, or constant cravingsgales hit. Jesus told Nicodemus, the Jewish teacher, that the kingdom of God is so "other" that we can't even see it unless we're born again (see John 3:3). Thankfully, as God's children and new creatures in Christ, we have his promise that we'll grow in holiness to be more like our King. What he has begun in us, he will complete because he is the author and perfecter of our faith (see Heb. 12:2).

So great is our King's love for us that he pursues us with a holy passion, calls us to himself by name, and ends our blindness. From there, we start a lifetime of learning what he looks like, walking in his footsteps, chasing after him like children. We long to find him as our

- *Creator.* He brings calm to our chaos and replaces despair with hope. Nothing can overpower God who loves us and wants his best for us. In this, we find peace.

- *Redeemer.* He removes guilt and condemnation from our records and replaces them with his unconditional love and acceptance in Christ. In this, we find forgiveness.

- *Preserver.* He holds us together and restores us in our weariness when we depend on him for everything and draw near to him through Christ. In this, we find rest.

- *Provider.* He fills us with eternal provisions that meet our needs and satisfy the longings of our hungry souls. In this, we find contentment.

- *Defender.* He goes before us, stands beside us, promises to never leave us nor forsake us even in our toughest battles. In this, we find courage.

- *Teacher.* He reveals himself to us through Christ and through his Word. He teaches us patiently with compassion and tenderness. In this, we find knowledge.

- *King.* He expresses his sovereign and gracious will in our lives. In his kingdom, the streets are paved with purity, and the walls are made of truth. Justice and love balance perfectly in his courtroom. His splendor, majesty, and holiness stir our hearts with gratitude and wonder. In this, we worship.

Even when we lose sight of God in the thick of our trials, he is never far off. In fact, when our circumstances are the most difficult and chaotic, he teaches us about who and where he really is. He involves himself in our lives, forgiving us, caring for us, teaching us the secrets of his heart.

Remembering a few basics about God can help you see him and find him when life's responsibilities and commitments cloud your view of him. When you learn what God looks like and where he is, you can find him in your chaos, mistakes, weariness, neediness, confusion, and battles. God is findable, not because you can pin him down or confine him to definitions of your own. God comes to you and makes himself known by his Holy Spirit through Christ because he loves you. Truth is the only reason we find God at any time, in any place, by any method, because he found us first.

AND THERE HE WAS . . .

by Nancy Cox

What do you do when everything you trusted God for is shattered, when your trust in the King of the universe feels as if it's been destroyed?

When I was a new Christian, I prayed, "Lord, I don't want to be a *soft-cushion* Christian. I want everything you have for me." At the age of twenty-nine and married with two small children, I realized that he'd heard my prayer.

My father was dying of a disease that slowly shut down his nervous system. My mother refused to accept help to care for him or to put him in a nursing home. Because she loved Dad so deeply, she cared for him but not for herself, and she wore out. The result was a chemical imbalance that lasted fifteen years.

We cared for my parents in their home for two months before moving them in with us. We watched my father slowly die and my mother become unable to function in society. Her condition caused her to do irrational things. For the ten years that Mom lived with us, we never knew what disaster would greet us each day. I didn't think God should allow such horrible things to happen to our family. *If this is what it's like to be a Christian,* I thought, *I'm not sure I want any part of it.* When I gave my life to the Lord, I thought things would go smoothly. Was I wrong!

Although I didn't understand it at the time, God wasn't tearing my faith down, but he was building it up through difficult circumstances. And he was teaching me to trust him as my sovereign Lord and King. I learned to take one day at a time and let its problems be enough. I committed everything to God in prayer, waited on his direction, and obeyed whatever he said to do even if it didn't make sense to me.

My faith grew strong. For twenty years, the Lord proved that even in hard times, he was there and in control. He gave me peace in the storm and a faith that didn't waiver. I prayed all the time about everything, especially about our children. "Lord, please don't let bad things happen to them. Please keep horrible things away from them."

Then God allowed one of our children to test the waters in a way I'd asked him to prevent. Something I had dreaded was now a part of our family's reality. It was one thing having to handle difficult situations with my parents, but it was another when it affected my children. I didn't know how to pray anymore. God seemed to have let me down. Everything I'd based my life on and taught my family was gone. My faith fell in ruins, and I asked, "What do I do now? What do I believe?"

For weeks I walked around aimlessly. I felt hopeless, unable to understand who God was, unable to pray. I was crushed, but I had a choice to make. I could continue to believe that God was good and able to care for his children or I could go back to the world's way of trusting in myself. Wrestling with this decision, I realized I had placed expectations on God. And when things didn't happen like I thought they should, I doubted him.

One day, I remembered the Bible said to keep the faith, to finish the race—every race God puts us in here on earth, not just the final race when life is over. God then gave me the strength and courage to keep going in our difficult situation.

I'd like to say things got easier. They didn't. But I decided to go on fighting against my flesh that wanted to run away from the pain, and against our enemy, the devil. I knew Satan wanted me to give up, but I wasn't going to let him have the victory. That's when the Lord showed me he was still there, that he was adding a new layer of faith to my life. My King knew what he was doing all the time.

God rekindled my faith, but I was still afraid that things would get worse for my child. Once again I had a choice to make. I could worry and wear myself out trying to handle things on my own, or I could believe that God would take care of them. I could not control the circumstances, but he could.

I've always admired Christians who say they never worry about anything—they just give their problems to God and let go. I could never do that. It was no different in my present situation. I constantly thought about the circumstances. *What if things don't change? Why did this happen anyway?* On my prayer walks, I poured my heart out to God, many times with tears and other times in anger. I told him I didn't understand what he was doing. But on one of my walks, Isaiah 46 kept turning over and over in my mind. I went home, grabbed my Bible, and then God showed me something I'd never seen before. "Their idols are borne by beasts of burden. The images that are carried about are burdensome, a burden for the weary. They stoop and bow down together; unable to rescue the burden, they themselves go off into captivity" (Isa. 46:1, 2 NIV).

Our child's situation had become a heavy burden. I could feel it bowling me over, holding me captive. I couldn't do anything without worrying about it, without dwelling on it. I knew the Bible said I was to have no gods other than the Lord. In my reluctance to accept God's sovereign care, had I lost sight of him, the real King over my life and my heart? Had our difficult circumstances become a false god that I worshiped through worry?

I desperately wanted to find God again, to sense his rule and reign in our situation, to believe he was using it for his glory and our good. But I didn't know how, that is, until he led me to this passage: "There is a river whose streams make glad the city of God, the holy place where the Most High dwells. God is within her, she will not fall; God will help her at break of day" (Ps. 46:4, 5 NIV).

As I read those verses, I knew I had to lay my worry down for good and run to the river where I'd receive strength to trust God to take care of things. I needed to remember that he alone is able to, because all power and authority belongs to him. He is the true God and my King.

Since those days, I understand that God allowed something difficult in my life, not to destroy my faith but to show me that worry was an idol that took away worship and praise from him. Sometimes I still struggle to cast all my cares on him, but when I do, I run to the river where his peace and power flow. He reminds me that he knows what he's doing even when I feel like he doesn't. He has been my good and gracious King through it all.